Trust Forgiveness Neighborly

Three Principles to Life

STUDENT and SERVANT

WESTBOW°
PRESS
A DIVISION OF THOMAS NELSON
& ZONDERVAN

Scripture quotations are from The Holy Bible, English Standard Version®
(ESV®), copyright © 2001 by Crossway, a publishing ministry of
Good News Publishers. Used by permission. All rights reserved.

WestBow Press books may be ordered through booksellers or by contacting:

WestBow Press
A Division of Thomas Nelson & Zondervan
1663 Liberty Drive
Bloomington, IN 47403
www.westbowpress.com
1 (866) 928-1240

Please send any comments or corrections to: TFN.Book@Gmail.com

Because of the dynamic nature of the Internet, any web addresses or
links contained in this book may have changed since publication and
may no longer be valid. The views expressed in this work are solely those
of the author and do not necessarily reflect the views of the publisher,
and the publisher hereby disclaims any responsibility for them.

Any people depicted in stock imagery provided by Thinkstock are
models, and such images are being used for illustrative purposes only.
Certain stock imagery © Thinkstock.

ISBN: 978-1-4908-2875-6 (sc)
ISBN: 978-1-4908-2874-9 (hc)
ISBN: 978-1-4908-2876-3 (e)

Library of Congress Control Number: 2014904005

Printed in the United States of America.

WestBow Press rev. date: 03/06/2014

Preface

The base concepts used in this book have been stated many different ways in many different cultures throughout the ages, but they always seemed to lack practical reasoning. This book adds the dimension of details to assist in understanding why these philosophies will work with examples. I chose to match up the core principle concepts with evidence to explain how they work. I have included alternative methods for understanding the process that governs our abilities with some scientific facts and references to where you can continue researching these topics. This book is for anyone who is ready to take a step toward learning how to live right and wants to understand the reasoning behind the force that drives us to act in certain ways. I compare reading this book to taking the red pill in the movie "The Matrix" as this book will open your eyes as you begin to see the truth that was hidden in front of you in plain sight. My hope is that this book will expand your understanding of what life is and how life works this way you can learn how to fill yourself up with love and good positive energy. My intention is to make this information available to everyone and touch as many people as conceivable possible. Most of all this is for my children, my wife and the rest of my family. We can make a huge change in the right direction if we all practice these principles. In order to help change along, we need to spread the message to as many people as possible. If the explanation and information makes sense, please pass it along so others around you can benefit. Eventually, the knowledge will grow. Perhaps, others may further the research and expand on the information in this book.

I started with one purpose in mind; that was to give to my children a thorough exposure to what I can best describe as the most fundamental aspect to understanding how we worked. As I continued adding to my notes, it was apparent that keeping any experiential knowledge that I have gained as a secret within my family was not brotherly in the cosmic understanding that we are all children of God. I therefore made a decision that I needed to write this in a way that it would be available to all. There are times where my writing and my focus may seem as though I am talking directly to my kids. I very well may be as I started off in that manner, but I want you to be conscious to the fact that I am also talking to everyone reading this book. It does not matter how old you are, the point is that you try to open your eyes and understand what is truly going on in life. Anyone can change their behaviors and live a more loving and happier life with a few adjustments to how they live.

I am not a professional book writer, some of that may come out in my writing and dialogue. That fact did not stop me from completing the writing of this book, as I know in my heart it is important to write this all down in a concise, to the point book. I have in the past talked myself right out of doing a good thing or not taking a chance based upon my lack of faith. For that reason, it is important for me to not give into fear or left brain over analysis that is based in any form for where the writing of this book could lead. I want to be free of the over rationalization that has so often in the past paralyzed me from doing something in the past. In order to do that, I had to subdue the rational thinking. I had to make it work for me and not I for it. Albert Einstein said *"The intuitive mind is a sacred gift and the rational mind is a faithful servant. We have created a society that honors the servant and has forgotten the gift".* The inner voice was one of our best assets, but we have forgotten how to use it. Therefore, I made the decision to publish this on faith alone that it will be beneficial and not just beneficial for my kids but to many. This book is available now for anyone to read. If you have an open mind and read through it in its entirety, something inside you will surely change for the better.

In the beginning, I started with just a few background concepts that can help us think about things in different ways and to point out some scientific facts. These facts are available for further examination and if you take the time to you search for more information, you will find it. I included this information in the event you need explanations or other facts to add additional validity or clarify some feelings and perceptions on things. At first some of this appears to be unexplainable, but if you look you will understand. I designed this first section in the book so that it would give you a basis from where to start searching if you choose to further investigate. This book should provide a solid foundation to show you how you can free yourself in a manner that allows for thinking outside the box, therefore providing the ability to look from outside to see what is in the box. I think this can be best thought of from a certain perspective as a new way to look within oneself. I hope you will see the value in this approach and build on it. While I organized the information in a format by gathering it and categorizing it, I worked very hard to evaluate the data based upon its own merits. If there is a perception that brews conflict with anything in the bible, the bible is to be taken as the ultimate authoritative truth on the subject in question. I wrote this book out of my faith in God and my love for all of you. Read below passage from bible explaining who and what God is.

1 John 4:7-8 ⁷Beloved, let us love one another, for love is from God, and whoever loves has been born of God and knows God. ⁸Anyone who does not love does not know God, because God is love.

For the same reason a doctor usually does not treat his close friends and family members or a therapist does not counsel his own family I remain nameless. This is due mainly to preconceived notions, prejudices and non beliefs of knowing the doctor or therapist. Usually there is not much good absorbed by the family and friends of doctors or counselors; they just do not make good patients.

Luke 4:23-24 ²³And he said to them, "Doubtless you will quote to me this proverb, 'Physician, heal yourself.' What we have heard you did at Capernaum, do here in your hometown as well." ²⁴And he said, "Truly, I say to you, no prophet is acceptable in his hometown.

When you go away on a vacation somewhere and are surrounded by unknown people, you can in essence be whoever you want to be as no one is tying you down to your past or how you acted before and therefore you can relax and be who you really are.

Reflection and Mission

As we grow older, it is apparent that we seem to live life in a more relaxed atmosphere realizing what we thought was important is not and what was not import really is. It can raise regrets that can even make us feel sad. Almost naturally, we base our decisions on lessons that we have learned firsthand. I realized that I had based my approach to handling many decisions as a parent and a role model all wrong. I made many mistakes, never realizing how lost I was as I navigated my way through life. Due to this realization, I knew that I had to find a way to fix these errors and provide a sound foundation with a knowledge base that contains the necessary tools to navigate through life without getting lost. I do have a purpose in writing this book. My main purpose is based on how important this is for me to share to my children and anyone who is looking to make sense of everything that happens in life. By my action to take the time to write this book if just some of this settles in, then a wonderful thing has happened. For my children, I want to create a memory that will be so ingrained that you will always remember there is a source to go to that contains information with truth in the interconnectivity to the universe in which we live. I want to provide this book in a format that could be used as a reference point, if you so choose to use it. I am thankful for the ability to reflect and use my many challenges in my life to gain understanding. I want to provide you with my experiences as a reference, so you will have the opportunity to make decisions with infinitely better results than mine were. By my sharing with you how we can be easily misled in life and destroy ourselves in the process, I hope it will help open your eyes so that you can find a better way. By identifying the situations I fell into, I hope you will be able to avoid many of the similar situations and live happier and free. Therefore, it is important for me to share the pitfalls and potholes I experienced so far in life so you will be aware of them and recognize the traps before you fall in.

As I was coming out of my sleep I was privileged to see how many stumbling blocks are placed everywhere, including in front of others closely around me. I will not spend too much time on them, as we all have to overcome the pitfalls in life we so often create for ourselves. What I will tell you, is that during my realization of what was actually happening around me, I was able to reach out to and assist some of them in recognizing that they need to look at their own behaviors and understand how it impacted the very situations in life they were dealing with. In so doing, they too have begun waking up. For others, I had no choice but to stand by and watch as they became so angry, so resentful, so self absorbed and so disconnected with living that their light inside dimmed. I pray that they see their ways and find an escape from the insanity in which it is leading them, especially those that were following their role model into the darkness. I feel for them, especially for those caught between a rock and a hard place. They did not know where to go. They solely relied on the illusion of happiness from their need to identify with the materialistic world.

It is a fact, that when you are disconnected and have the wrong belief system anyone can go off track. It is a gift when one can get a bird's eye view to look from high above the direction they are heading and see a way back to the right path to get themself where they need to go. I want you to know that even if you do get lost, there is always a way out and a way to get back on track. I know this to be true by so many different experiences in life. Some near me in my inner circle knew all too well what was going on. Others judged me for their own feelings of inadequacy and further pushed me down. Regardless of the process and how I ended up, most of it was well deserved in a way and a blessing in disguise. During the dark times, I grew further disconnected from life. I was bitter, upset and did not know to the degree that I was disconnected and suffering. I somehow instinctively knew that in order turn around I needed to get reattached to God and the church was the best way. I remember having my family and others pray for me. Through this process and the faith I still had, something happened to me. I was able to lean on my faith and trust it enough to feel a change. It was almost instantaneous, as I started to see things and understand things I could not before. To be philosophical as well as literal, I started to see a light at the end of the tunnel. I followed the light as I left the cold bitter darkness behind. This was very important, as it helped solidify in my mind that faith and love can overcome anything and everything. I was reminded where the true power is, therefore I want to provide you with a reference to what I have learned in a way that you can always find it and use it. This book is great to read from beginning to end, but it can also be used as a guide, a reference or a reminder to help you as you grow up in life. After overcoming many tribulations in my life and realizing the direct correlation to my beliefs and my state of mind, I realized that anyone can overcome anything with the right tools. I wanted to make sure you knew what tools are good for you and will never fail when applied properly in life.

I had a mission, which was to make this as simple to understand as well as offer you some methods for relating to and understanding how these things are interconnected. I wanted to show you how everything makes sense when you can open your mind to understanding and find ways to seeing how spirituality and science can help solidify concepts in each other. In order to truly benefit from the information, we have to relax the constraints of only accepting reality as what we can see. It was important to give you a high level introduction in as short of form as possible and still get the important concepts through. I wanted to emphasize the importance of the written word found in the bible and how it does tell us the same things we are explaining in the various fields of science. There is so much more to understand that is available if you pursue knowledge and wisdom, but you have to want it. I do not have all the answers. I do know if I ask God, that God will reveal to me the appropriate understanding to the question in a way that I can understand. I want you to understand that you too have this available if you truly believe and ask, but you have to know what to believe in. This why it was important to share with you how with just three simple principles when followed will guarantee a more fulfilling life.

Energy, Spirit and its influences

Throughout life we must strive to do what is right and not be led away from that purpose. I want to state that I am firm believer in wisdom. Sometimes this wisdom is hidden right before our very eyes in the way of catchy phrases or in ancient writings. Most notably the words of wisdom found in the bible are filled with knowledge and understanding on many levels of consciousness. Many great Saints, philosophers and highly intellectually gifted people have been saying similar ideas and implied certain principles should be followed in life. For instance, Nikola Telsa stated "'If you want to find the secrets of the universe, think in terms of energy, frequency and vibration". I will reference similar statements or writings from time to time as I get into facets of understanding that will help unlock different ways to think. Please keep an open mind and listen to what I say in its entirety before you make any decision on any information. William Paley wrote this quote "The infidelity of the Gentile world, and that more especially of men of rank and learning in it, is resolved into a principle which, in my judgment, will account for the inefficacy of any argument, or any evidence whatever, *viz.* contempt prior to examination." What this quote is saying and has been utilized by many famous people in history is the way to keep yourself ignorant is to discount what someone is stating prior to hearing all of what they said.

I want to begin with some background facts that will lay the foundation for these three principles. There are forces or influences all around us that have the ability to impact and assist us in choosing the right or wrong path to follow. It is important to know good sources so you can have them ready when you need them. It is also important to know about other sources that can impact your decisions in choosing the right path. In knowing and being aware of these influences one can be better prepared when exercising their free will and making choices in life. Not knowing about these influences can lead a person into making decisions through ignorance which may lead a person to death, metaphorically and literally. I state this because I was on a path to certain death both physically and spirituality. That discussion can happen at a later time.

I want to give you basic concepts that are important to understanding the world in which we live. We should first understand that everything is truly energy in one form or another. If we look at the definition of force, it is strength or energy as an attribute of physical action or movement; coercion or compulsion; push or pull on an object resulting from the objects interaction with another object. Spirit is defined as the vital principle or animating force within living beings. Spirit can be thought of as a power derived from principles. By having good or bad principles, you can generate positive or negative forces that influence attitudes and behaviors. Showing your team spirit by cheering and supporting them with positive affirmations is a common method for transferring spiritual source energy to a destination. The team benefits by receiving positive energetic thoughts that can be converted and used in a way to motivate the team to play hard. The core underlining understanding that defines Spirit, power and energy are very similar. Keep that in mind as it is important in understanding what I want you to know.

If you understand this information and verify the truth behind it simply by basing it on its own merits, then it is important that we make the obvious decision to surround ourselves with good positive loving forms of energy. Since we are given free will, we should use that free will to seek out good energy influences and steer clear of bad energy influences. Understanding the energy influences around us and how that energy can impact our emotions is best accomplished with some thinking outside the box. I can honestly say that everything can be thought of as energy. Einstein's famous equation of $E=MC^2$ is the mathematical formula that substantiates the interchangeability of energy and mass. We currently are immersed in a universe that uses energy in many different forms. We are designed to sense the different forms of energy around us through the various sensory organs connected to our body. Sound for example is energy. The energy emitted from sound travels in vibrations or waves that sometimes we can also feel with our body. In this first part, I will focus on our ears and sensing energy though sound waves. Sound in the way of certain combinations of musical tones can give us an uplifted feeling inside. Music can make us feel like dancing or it can make us feel like running that extra mile or persevering through tough times. Music has a magical ability in the way it can make us feel.

Most people are unaware that even if we are unable to consciously hear the music or various sounds, if it is playing around us it will still impact our emotions. To truly understand what I am saying, a little bit of wisdom is needed here. The normal human hearing has the ability to hear consciously a certain range of sounds. When the sound energy is out of that range you consciously do not hear it, but your subconscious still hears it. What surprised me is that when the sound is not consciously listened to, it bypasses your conscious listening. When this subconscious listening occurs, there is no filter whereby someone can choose to listen to something else by changing the station, turning it off or leaving the area. Without the filter, you are not consciously aware of the sound. That means the sound goes directly into your subconscious. This will have a profound effect, especially if the sound energy is negative. Scientist, the military and government know about this and how it can be used to control groups of people. This usage of sound wave energy is known as a form of mind control most notably known as subliminal messaging. When it is so low that you are unable to consciously hear it, they label it as silent subliminal mind control. I am not about delving into conspiracy theories. I just want to present the information for the purpose of explaining the different forms of energy. I do not want to deviate too much here, you can research all this on your own as there is countless articles and books written on the subject. Just know that it is real and it is happening.

On a side note, I read recently about the possibility that original secret Solfeggio frequencies used in ancient music have been rediscovered. It was said to have been buried in the bible for over 3,000 years. The sound waves generated using these tones have abilities to heal and levitate objects that science is just discovering is possible with certain frequencies of sound waves. These sounds have profound effects on nature and people, especially in emotions. If you take the time to research you can now find music played with these rediscovered frequencies tuned into the instruments. I have not personally done much research in this area, but is worth looking into.

Besides music's capacity to make us feel upbeat, music also has the ability to make us feel scared, tired, angry, restless, discontent, and many other emotions. We can best see the use of sound in this manner within most horror movies. At certain scenes in the movie, they change the music theme to something loud with a low frequency and out of key to set our emotions into a worrisome stressful state. They want us to be sitting at the end of our seats in a fearful reactionary mode so that we are highly susceptible to being scared. Movie directors and producers hire and use the best sound and video technology to get the right response from their audience. They are quite successful in achieving their goals in a short period of time. They bring us through a wide range of emotions throughout the movie they created.

Since I mentioned movies, let us also look at energy in the form of light waves too. Light is energy and we are able to perceive the light energy in different ways. Intense light can give off warmth, but let us for now focus on visible light waves and how we use our eyes to interpret light signals. We receive the light and it has encoded within it the packets of light wave information in the form of cohesive images that we recognize. Understanding the basic process that we convert light waves into information is all that is really needed at this point. The same way that music can impact us when we use our senses to listen and interpret the energy with our ears, when we look at a picture or watch a video it can have the same type of effects. For most people, looking at a picture of a baby smiling or a puppy dog playing impacts our emotions in a good way. When we look at something like pain and suffering it has a different effect on our emotions. Some can tear at our insides as we can feel the pain simply by looking at certain images of suffering. A simple photograph can make us feel sad and even impact our decisions. There is a range of emotions that images have on our emotions. These are very basic examples but that is all that is needed to get the point across. There are countless articles on pictures and videos impacting our emotions if you want to research this more, but again just know that this is true and is happening daily. My only goal was to highlight a couple basic forms of energy that we are immersed in and to point out how light waves as interpreted by our brains will have an impact on our emotions. As long as the picture or video we are looking at is clear and nothing is hidden, we can see everything in it consciously. As long as we are conscious of the entire image, we have the ability to filter out or turn away from something negative. The sad truth though, is that many images have hidden meanings or pictures hidden within an image or movie in some way. Our subconscious understands everything immediately. Our subconscious recognizes patterns and hidden images so we again have the same issue as with hearing. We have subliminal messages going directly to our subconscious through images or video.

Many advertisements and commercials use hidden meanings in their arrangement of actors and products. They concentrate their approach to make us feel like we have to purchase certain products or services. They normally create an environment of excitement and a feeling of necessity to act now. As a matter of fact, one of the most important sales tactics used by anyone selling a good or service is to create the feeling that a person needs that item now by creating a sense of urgency. The sales person's job is to make the buyer believe if they do not buy it right now, they will never get that same deal again. It is dishonest in a way, deep down we all know that given enough time the same price and quite possibly even a lower price will be available again. Time and time again, people fall for that illusion and spend money on things they do not need and later have buyer's remorse. If only they knew the truth they would not feel so pressed to make a decision on the spot. The same is true about the subliminal messaging and energy influences all around us, we just need to know what is going on.

I do wonder if I knew early in life what I know now how things may have turned out. The idea of having 20-20 hindsight vision would have been nice. However, I do prefer that I am able to create this guide for you as I prefer to be the one that had to suffer. Had I avoided the many pitfalls, I may not have learned as much as I have. Know that you do not have to go through hard lessons in life, which is what I did. At the same time I am not hampering your free will. Everyone must learn in whatever way is best for them. However, knowing what I know now is why I try to minimize your exposure to violent video games and vulgar music as I want to completely eliminate your exposure to those negative influences. More importantly, I want to eliminate your interest in being exposed to that garbage and to be a choice that you make on your own as it will only get more challenging as you get older. Now is a good time to train and test your will power to choose wisely since you are being educated on it effects through this book.

Let me also continue expand other methods besides sound, pictures and video. Books are unique as they fall within the scope of visible light energy, auditory (if listening to them) and even touch if the person is blind and reading the book in Braille. All three methods for receiving energy from books will have an impact on our emotions and feelings. Books regardless of whether we are consciously aware they are fiction or non-fiction will still impact us the same way as it generates an appropriate emotional response based upon the material in the book. Videos, pictures and music also have the same impact to our emotions as we have discussed. This dilemma is due to the realization that our subconscious does not understand what is real or not real, to it everything is considered real. Every experience whether it is a video, movie or book adds information to our experience in life. This is important to understand, but we will stay focused on books for now. Every book you absorb, regardless of the methods you expose yourself to it will impact your beliefs, emotions and experiences. Subliminal messaging can enter our subconscious without our conscious being aware of it in books, much the same way it happens in music, pictures or videos. Inside many sacred writings, there are codes hidden and embedded all over. Sometimes there are entire books hidden within books. These hidden books go mostly un-noticed by our conscious mind. Our subconscious on the other hand understands and absorbs this information and incorporates it into our daily life and belief systems unconditionally. As we read these books it impacts our emotions the same way as sound energy and light energy does. Reading is just another vehicle used to sense energy. We then interpret it into information for our mind to process and absorb. Sometimes, you can see or understand consciously the hidden meaning of the writings simply by re-exposure over and over to the same data. Each subsequent download into our subconscious mind opens up the door little by little to greater wisdom and knowledge.

When certain writings are understood, it will dramatically alter how you look at everything around you. It will change the very essence of how you live life. One such collection of books that I have drawn wisdom from is the bible. If you take the time to read and study its works, you will find that not only consciously you see things written and understand, but subconsciously the hidden books, patterns and code in the bible will be absorbed into your experience of life. What I found is that the bible can both literally and philosophically put an end to death and create life. The bible is a place to seek refuge, protection and guidance when all else seems to fail. This book has meanings in literal forms, philosophical and imbedded codes. I do not want to deviate too much into the topic of hidden meanings or secret codes in the bible, however some of the code in the bible has been deciphered and patterns have been found. Perhaps other higher level patterns need to be incorporated to find more. Maybe a pattern like the Fibonacci sequence as it approaches Phi ratio could unlock more. This I do not know for sure, I only show it as an example of how outside the box thinking is needed to unlock secrets and codes. I only look at reasoning, that any code must also have the information to break the code embedded in a way that one can understand. What is told to us within the context of the bible is that God is the Alpha and Omega, beginning and the end. Since the Fibonacci begins with zero and approaches the Phi ratio which is known as the "Golden ratio" or "Perfect ratio" that maybe using this type of sequence is the code needed to unlock more secrets found within the bible.

The main point I wanted to make and I want you to understand is that seemingly harmless activity on the surface may have a dramatic impact on our well being. I learned that we need to be aware of flashing lights. Flashing lights whether in specific patterns or seemingly random fluctuations impact our emotions and mental processes. The flashes of light are used in treatment for certain neurological conditions. Flashing lights also cause some people to have adverse reactions, like seizures. I only want to make sure you are aware of and understand the facts as to how subtle energy all around us will impact us. Again, there are ample books and articles on the subject of flashing light waves. My goal is to only expose you to this way of thinking. I want you to know that all is not what it seems many times.

We can also sense and interpret light waves beyond the visible spectrum. Unless we are looking for these light waves we would not know they were around us. Take for example the ultra violet light waves, X rays, infrared. Different frequencies and wave length cause the energy to go from harmless visible light to dangerous forms of invisible radiation. We can even die from exposure to the wrong range of the photons that make up these light waves, I do not know enough on this subject so I do not want to try to expand too much here.

I point much of this out so that you too will think outside the box when exposed to certain situations. Seemingly innocent naming conventions or mistakes in the way things are named may not be so innocent. For instance, if there was some force that wanted to persuade people to do bad things, one way would be to take the names good things and assign them to what is not good in order to fool people into taking what is not good. Also take the names of what is not good and link them to names of what is good in order to fool people to stay away from what is really good. Therefore, with minimal effort people would just do bad things like exposing themselves to bad things thinking it has no impact on them. If you think about it, just because something feels good or taste good, does not mean it is good for you. For anyone can add sugar to poison to hide the taste. This is why we must stay resilient.

Most everyone, if they knew something will hurt them would try to stay away from it. Stay aware of your surroundings and your emotions. We have the ability to sense our surroundings and realize if something is bad for us. It is harder when the effects take a while, but that is where you need to pay attention and make choices of what you want to expose yourself to. It is obvious that the faster the realization of the pain, the faster you would respond to a bad situation and get away from it. Look at how well we get the message from a hot stove. As soon as you touch it and get burned, you instantaneously realize the damage it is doing you so you pull your hand away quickly. What is not so obvious is exposure to bad energy, it is subtle as it takes a while to build up and cause problems. We all know that over time smoking builds up tar and causes health issues. It took a long time to realize the problems and accept the evidence of problems, like cancer as truth. Society did not want to hear that something they enjoyed could be bad for them. We love to rationalize and justify problems so we can continue to justify behavior we do not want to let go of. We continue the behavior until it is unavoidable and we must accept the facts based upon observations that the behavior is the source of the problem. The same is true for what we surround ourselves with in life. Most of us knowingly would not want to surround ourselves with bad things if we knew they were bad. For years the tobacco companies kept telling us smoking is non-addictive and does not cause health problems. For a long time, society was willing to believe this lie. It was the perfect lie. It prevented people from facing up to the truth and giving up something they had been used to doing. This brings me to a passage in the bible:

Isaiah 5:20 - [20] *Woe unto them that call evil good, and good evil; that count darkness as light, and light as darkness; that put bitter for sweet, and sweet for bitter!*

This seemingly little passage explains quite a bit about what is wrong with our world. We have been fooled and so confused about what is truly important in life. We are growing up in a culture that further propagates a false belief that success is based on identity and materialistic things and therefore how we act in life is not that important. Everywhere we look people are so engrossed with this false belief, further confirming the lie in which we are living to ourselves. It makes it hard to go against the grain and see the truth. The hard fact is that we have accepted the lie as truth. When we are so immersed in this lifestyle, it is challenging to understand what is true and whether we are going in the right direction or not. It requires the determination to look at ourselves as a whole, the good and the bad. We need to reflect and realize what our part was in these experiences. We need to know where we have been, where we are now and based upon these variables, will we get where we want to be or do we need a new map?

In order to get an accurate assessment, we have to be willing to gauge our progress with honesty. We have to truly look within ourselves and not outside to see the truth. In order to accomplish this, you have to pull yourself out of the chaos so you can look at everything from the eye of an observer with no preconceived ideas or philosophies and then be willing to accept the truth that reveals itself to you. I had to take an honest inventory of myself and how my behaviors and actions manifested certain events in my life. I evaluated and thought to myself, "Is this what my five year old self wanted to be doing?". By looking at who I wanted to be and what I wanted to do when I was younger, it gave me the opportunity to review what events in my life changed. When I was younger, I had fantastic ideas and no preconceived notions about what is possible. I just knew what felt right and let my heart direct me. I was quite happy when I was very young. As I started school and was exposed to influences and other ideas from my peers so things changed. The changes start out subtle, but the fact is that I was exposed to many things that began altering my direction. This is what I want you to be aware of, the subtle influences in life that will alter your direction. I am not saying that changing one's mind is a bad thing, but when that change is made unaware do to exposure to the wrong type of energy, it can have a dramatic impact on your future.

I never knew that the influences of other people, places and things were changing my beliefs. It changed them so much that until recently I did not know it had even occurred or let alone when it began. I call that phase, the sleep phase. I was just going through the motions in life, completely unaware that I was not living life true to my core self, my spiritual self. I was "sleep walking" and living life according to the people, places and things in which I had surrounded myself with. Another way to think about this was that I was a passenger in my own body. I wasn't driving my body, something else was.

My true inner self was trying to wake me up constantly, by sending me signals in different ways. I had many events and experiences in life that could have opened my eyes had I been paying attention. I just assumed life was being life. I assumed that many of us are victims and we just live it. I never realized that my actions, beliefs and thoughts were impacting the very interaction I experienced with life. For some of us who are lucky, we eventually do wake up. I want that to happen for you now. The sooner in life you realize this, the better a life you will create for yourself. Once you wake up and see the truth for what it is, you change and you begin the process of making better decisions. You will no longer be in a daze, or asleep. You will be more focused on what you are willing to expose yourself to and make the choices to leave situations that pull you down. You will be dedicated to insuring your surroundings are in sync with what is good and truly important to you in life. Remember, the choice is yours. When you make the right choices in life, you truly have the ability to do whatever you want to do and be free. Choose wisely and live life in a way that you will be true to yourself. Use the right tools to navigate through life in a way to keep you on course.

There are still other less obvious energy based forms of influence on us that we are in constant contact with all the time. Gravity and magnetism impacts our thinking and moods. There is a documented effect on human behavior related to the moons gravitational effect on our thinking. Go around and ask any police officer and hospital staff if they notice any difference in activity around a full moon and their answer is most often yes. There is scientific backing to human behavior changes linked to the location of the stars and planets. It is based upon the subtle differences in gravitation these celestial bodies have on us, the metals and changes in electrical activity in our brains. Again there are books and other materials on this subject of gravitational forces and human behavior.

Magnetism also impacts our thinking and emotional well being. It has been proven scientifically and is used in medical therapies. One recent new, widely utilized procedure is called transcranial magnetic stimulation. This process is currently utilized for treating depression by depolarizing or hyper polarization of specific neurons in the brain. Both of these forces of energy are very real and very hard to tell that they exist in subtle doses. In other words, these forces can impact your very thoughts and emotions while at the same time, you are not completely aware of their presence all around you. As you realize this fact, you do begin to stay alert and more aware of their presence. This is why it is important to educate yourself with as much information as possible. Simply knowing that these forms of energies can influence our thinking should give you a new perspective on why sometimes we feel certain ways in certain places or around certain people or places. Knowing this empowers you in many ways. It reminds us that we have the ability to change our surroundings when we get a "gut" feeling or are feeling lousy inexplicably. For example, if your emotions suddenly change in an unexplainable way, try to see if there is a source that you can identify that may be causing this change. Move away from it or change what you are doing, watching, reading or listening to. You may be surprised at how the simple realization that there may be an energy source in your vicinity impacting your feelings can help you live a better life and live the right way.

Always remember that you have the power to eliminate contact with negative energy so it no longer can impact your life. Don't discount those "gut" feelings. Sometimes, the feeling may be coming from another person. You may get bad "vibes" from someone or goose pumps in severe cases, maybe dizziness or extreme fatigue. Your gut is trying to tell you something is wrong and to stay away from that person, but it could also be a place or thing. I was unaware for such a long time that this was happening to me. As a society, we just forgot how to read the cues. We have been told by many to ignore these things and that it is all in our head. We repeat this to our kids, to ignore these things as it is not real. Do you see the parody in that the negative forces have influenced us by telling us to ignore it all? The negative forces do not want us aware of their influence on us. We have been made to feel awkward if we acknowledge these gut feelings, again negative forces influencing us so we ignore it. As you grow you will encounter plenty of these "gut" feelings and hopefully you will trust them better than I did. If a person or group of people in your immediate vicinity is full of negativity, or electrified with bad energy in some way, most likely it is emanating from their heart(s) and mind(s). I do not want to go too far into the unseen forces at this point, but know they exist. Proof is gravity and magnetism in itself, we can only see the results of the force and not the force itself. We cannot see the energy field surrounding magnets or the earth as I am standing on it, but I know that force is pulling me to the ground. We also cannot see consciousness, but I know it exists as I am aware of myself as a conscious being. Here is a couple passages from the bible on what is unseen.

Hebrews 11:3 [3] *By faith we understand that the universe was created by the word of God, so that what is seen was not made out of things that are visible.*

2 Corinthians 4:18 [18] *as we look not to the things that are seen but to the things that are unseen. For the things that are seen are transient, but the things that are unseen are eternal.*

My goal in bringing these facts together on energy and its influences is to point out how factually based these influences are in our everyday life. The influences are documented throughout textbooks and videos. I want to give you reasons to think outside of the box and sense more than what the eye can see. If we look at the results, we can figure out that there must be influences by way of the results. Always thinking that we need to see the proof first, will keep us from seeing what is truly real with other sensory organs that we have available. We depend on our eyes the most and yet it is not the most powerful sensory organ. We cannot see though a solid wood door, but yet we can hear the sound on the other side. We cannot see through a solid steel door, but yet we can feel the temperature from the other side of the door. Of all the various forms of light waves, the visible spectrum is the smallest. We have been taught to rely solely on our sight and I tell you that our sight can keep us in the dark and blind to what is truly real.

It is time to get out of bed, wake up and do something to change your way of thinking. No battle or war has to be fought. Only an internal realization and a desire to remain true to our real self buried within us, is all that is required. I want you to wake up to see what is around us all the time and what we need to be aware of. To understand the real truth from the lies, we just have to be willing to open our eyes. To understand why the truth is so well hidden, one must think about what one loses if the truth was known as it will see a man free. It was once said the best place to hide something is in plain sight. That is what we are dealing with, the deceitful trickery we are exposed to all around. I want to reiterate the idea that mislabeling good from bad, truth from lies can keep a person ignorant.

Nobody wants to be the person that stands out against the grain, but that is what we must do in order to live life the right way. What we are up against is the fact that most everyone is asleep around us. Fearing ridicule and potential isolation keeps many from stating the facts and sometimes from even changing their beliefs. They would rather believe lies so as to not shake their very essence of living. They prefer to remain in ignorance and not admit anything openly in public for fear of ridicule or isolation. The fear of ridicule is a powerful tool if you want to keep someone believing something is not real, like the existence of unseen forces. Remember this throughout life; what could someone gain by making you believe or disbelieve a certain philosophy? It is important to weigh in a person's motives for selling a belief system. In making a decision on whether to change a belief after you have all the facts, evaluate which belief system is limiting or could be used to control you to act in specific ways. The best lie would be one that uses fear or peer pressure in a way that not believing it insures ridicule thereby self propagating the same lie. The culture we live in is geared towards making us live in fear and in a stressed out environment. We need to shift more toward living in a more loving way to each other if we want to gain a higher level of consciousness and understanding of one another.

There are studies that show there is a possibility of 64 genetic codes combination of amino acids in our DNA structure, but only 20 are active. When they mapped the patterns of the frequencies from our emotions, they realized that if we are emitting on a full frequency of pure unconditional love that all 64 of the connection points in our DNA linked up to the amino acids at the various connection points. When we live in fear, the frequency vibrates at a much lower rate and less contact points to the amino acids are made. Currently only 20 of the possible connection points are active. Frequency and vibration are forms of energy. The experiments and data show that love is a higher frequency and therefore has more power than fear as it allows for 64 connection points. In other words, there is a benefit for negative energies to make us try to live in fear. By doing so, it keeps our potential energy restrained. What we need to do is stop living in fear and just start living. In order to do that, it is important to be confident in your true beliefs and lead the way by always doing what is right. It is easier to go with the crowd than against it, but know that is not always the right path to choose especially when you realize it is time to change direction for the better. This is where knowing what is right and doing what is right will keep you clean and truly living.

Course correction

I want to come right out and state the obvious, in life I have made many mistakes. These mistakes caused many difficulties for not just me, but for those around me who loved me and who I loved. These errors I made or bad behaviors I was doing, I had to hide. I was not acting true to myself, and I did not want to let people around me really know what I was doing. I had to hide my behaviors and cover them up. Another way to think about these mistakes or errors in judgment is that they caused me to feel dirty as I tarnished myself. In other words, the spiritual power and energy inside me had become filthy or unclean. That dirty power source clogged my energy flow in my physical body from functioning correctly. It impacted my thoughts and how I felt. Even my overall health was impacted. I had started taking medications to help me think, focus and feel. I later learned that most, almost 70% of illnesses are what they call psychosomatic illnesses, which means they originate in the mind. This is one reason why the placebo effect exists. Further evidence in this area done by Candice Pert proved linkages between the mind and its state of emotions with your nervous, endocrine, immune and digestive systems. I recommend researching her work as she explains how neuropeptides transmit information throughout your body down to the cellular level. Information that originates from your everyday thoughts and feelings is transmitted through biochemical reactions originating from the mental and emotional stimuli you expose yourself too. These reactions occur often simultaneously in virtually every system of your body at once. Prolonged exposure to the wrong stimuli can lead to serious health problems. What is worse is that your body may become addicted to the wrong stimuli through repeated prolonged exposure. Your body learns to function with that negative exposure, so now it will try to keep you exposed to the wrong stimuli by sending you feelings of desire for things you should eliminate.

The research available in this area is amazing. It shows a direct link to how stress, anger and basically any negative emotions cause health problems. When your body is not getting what it needs, it is time to slow down and change what you are exposed to. If you don't, eventually your body will crash physically or mentally and make you slow down. These health issues are all reversible by many different natural ways. She found that energy vibrations impact the functioning of these biochemical processes and found a linkage to the benefits of sound therapy. Simply put, by changing lifestyles, adding meditation, music, living happier and unloading all the negativity in your life you can help heal yourself with no medications, permanently the right way. Add to this a change of activity, like exercise and eating healthier and the effects are miraculous.

Sometimes that negative stimuli impacting your well being is simply the energy from the attitudes of the people around you and how they see you. Without people even saying a word to you, just simply how they perceive you will influence your health. Their beliefs as to who you are, is usually based upon past behaviors. How we behaved and acted around them before is our fault and we must recognize that. However, that means that based upon our past behaviors then the very people we surround ourselves with can keep or make us sick through their thoughts. Their expectations of who we are in some way pull us towards fulfilling that expectation, even if it is a negative expectation. When they see us in a certain way, they can influence our very health and emotions. For instance, if they always see us as obese and over eating, most likely we will continue to over eat and be obese. If they see us as mentally ill, depressed, alcoholic or addicted to certain behaviors we then unconsciously are drawn to fulfilling their thoughts and meeting their expectations. When you realize and accept this fact, you will be more inclined to be careful with whom you surround yourself with. This is why to make a big change in your lifestyle, you may temporarily need to separate from the influences of people around you until you make that transition and be who you want to be. You need to be confident enough in who you are so that you change their beliefs as to who you are.

It works both ways, you want to give people a chance and not apply prejudices to people, especially when they are trying to make a change. If we are not aware of the interaction that our thoughts and expectations have on others, then we can unknowingly impact and cause other people to be sick. Our careless negative thoughts about someone, needs to be purged so we can give others a chance to be better too. Do your best to stay away from judging or talking bad about people. Try to see someone at their best, see them as you want them to be and pray for that to happen for them. Do not accept that they are condemned to be stuck in any particular condition as anything is possible with God. As much as you may want to talk about somebody's health condition, try not to as by doing so it further solidifies in your mind their current condition. By talking to many people, it spreads that persons health condition to other people's minds further hardening the belief to everyone around the health state of that person. Instead believe that whatever the health condition is, that it is gone and has been healed through prayer and meditation. This is the true way to help someone, using positive thoughts and emotions. I am not saying to ignore them if they ask for and clearly need help in some way. What I am saying is to not mentally dwell on the negative situation as you unknowingly add emotion and belief to the idea that they are permanently stuck that way. Some people are unaware of this influence. Some sick people are not in a position to move away from this type of exposure, be especially sensitive to them and only think positive thoughts or send them prayers and love.

When you decide that you want to change yourself for the better, it may be necessary to detox and withdraw from the bad stimuli. It may be best to disconnect from any negative people, places and things around you while you are transitioning. You need to pray and accept the ability given to us from God to change for the better. You may have new physical and emotional feelings during the transition phase. Push through it for a short period of time and your body will change. Once you fully accept the change and you believe it, you can then begin to reconnect with people, places and things that make logical sense to bring back into your life. Since you have the ability to make the choice to eliminate the exposure to negative stimuli from your environment, choose wisely. Do not fall into the lure of labeling someone as negative just so you do not have to face them for your own personal reasons. Truly look at each person and whether they impact you in a good or bad way. Don't be afraid to explain how all this works to those around you. Realize that faith and belief add to the power of thought and you can help people around you and also help yourself all at the same time if those people around you are open to listening. Thanks to free will, you can choose who and what you want to be exposed to, so be prudent in your decisions.

When I had finally taken the time to slow down and truly look at myself, I discovered that I was surrounding myself with negative people, places and things and therefore my health was deteriorating. I kept attracting more bad things into my life as my behavior was indicative of nurturing and developing bad habits. I was living in disharmony, out of tune with life. As things continued to grow further out of sync and out of tune I had to find ways to further mask what was inside me. I built up identity on top of identity to the point that I almost forgot who I was. It seemed that nothing was easy for me, that everything always went wrong. It seemed that no one could understand me. My life was out of my control. The more I tried to control it, the more that concept seemed to slip through my very finger tips. I was filled with so much anger, resentment and frustration with life that it was hard for me to not justify my "questionable" behavior. I fell into a pattern of not making good choices, as time went on the choices became worse. I became the very thing I so much did not want to be, a slave. I was no longer in control of my life as I was a slave to negative energies. The bible clearly identifies this as being a slave to sin. This is repeated many times in different passages in the bible. I recommend searching them out to read so you can look at all the circumstances and recurrences of the underlying theme. I figure when something is repeated several times, it must be very important. Here it is stated in John chapter 8 very clear and I advocate reading the entire passage on the children of Abraham.

John 8:34 - ³⁴ Jesus answered, "I assure you that everyone who sins is a slave to sin.

It is due to this fact that as much as I wanted to be in control of my life, I slowly was losing control. I was "selling" it away and no longer was in control of my life. Another way to think about this was that I was mortgaging out my soul and incurring such a large debt in the way of the guilt from sin. In order to pay the interest

I had to keep borrowing more and more by committing more sins, it is a vicious cycle. This sick course of action just happens without giving too much thought of the repercussions. When we lie, we seem to have to perpetuate additional lies to keep the original lie from being uncovered. As we do this, we sometimes create additional layers of false identities that we build up around us, especially if the lie has to do with covering up who we really are. We keep perpetuating more lies and justify them each time more and more. We are just incurring more and more guilt or debt from sin.

We all know where excessive debt leads us. It leads us into bankruptcy where we have nothing left. I want to provide direction to you that will help you with life overall and keep you debt free or guilt free. Understand too, that just because you may not feel guilty for doing something, you know in your heart it is wrong so you still accumulate sin debt. It is a blessing to feel guilt. Guilt just makes you aware of the debt that you have to payback. There are those that have become desensitized to guilt as they have accumulated so many sins and never cleansed themselves from it. Pray for them that they see the error in their ways.

Nobody wants to be a slave to another as we all want to be free. By being a slave, we risk being mistreated and we lose the ability to do what we really want to do. In order to maintain the freedom we all seek, you must be aware of how you behave and interact with people, places and things. What I am attempting to do, is to keep this explanation as short as possible. If I can provide you with enough evidence so that the evidence itself wakes you up and you open your eyes, it is a miraculous gift that will reap rewards far beyond comprehension. At the same time, you will know how and where to get more knowledge and wisdom as I am referencing my sources. The information gathered together will also help provide you with guidance for many decisions you will need to make. I pray that you will understand and see what is imperative to know in life in order to keep yourself safe. This too, will assist you with any difficult times you may encounter.

This book can work as a road map if you let it. Anytime you are lost and need to find your way back to truth, know that this book is a great resource. This book will help you find your way back to living and provide guidance if it is needed. Knowing where to look and how to decipher the facts is a skill that once your eyes are open, you will develop and fine tune. Knowing fact from fiction or knowing what is truly good from mislabeled bad information is critical to life. I searched and studied many philosophies my entire life, constantly searching for answers. To my surprise, what I needed was right in front of me the whole time. If I had opened my eyes and understood what was in front of me back then, I wonder where I would be right now. Although for me, I had to go through life in the way I did as I am hard headed and very independent. For someone like me, it took a lot to get through my false identities and pierce my heart and mind. Fortunately, when the light penetrated the darkness, I was able to see clearly in all directions. Because of this, I see how the various roads can lead you into two very distinctive paths and it is important for me to share with you how it happened to me. I unknowingly charted the waters toward darkness and on the way found the path toward light. For that, I am truly grateful and I want to share the map with you.

I want you to know that I have had many hard lessons and therefore faced my own challenges. You must know that it does not have to be that way for you. Let this book be like a map insert that provides you with direction and where to find the complete map. This is the true reason as to why I took the time to document what I learned. I do not want you to have to "re-invent the wheel". I want you to have a basis to learn and grow from. As I am continuing my learning and growing, I may add a second book as I am only pointing out critical components in this book. My goal is to make the information short and simple to understand so that you can easily absorb the truth. The quest for understanding and truth is where it all began for me. Situations all around me never quite added up. It just seemed out of place and out of sync. There are countless sources of quality information, but much of it is mixed up with opinions and leaves out the sources or what to look for if you want more facts. I wanted to provide you with the facts and where you can look to find more information to continue learning the truth. I consider myself a student and a servant. As a student, I want to share with you what I learned so we can continue to learn and grow together. As a servant I want to help you have the best opportunity at understanding what is real, truth and what will let you live. I believe that when you realize the truth about how to live, you will engage in a lifestyle that many want, but few understand how to get. I believe that if you continue searching for facts, you will continue learning more truths as wells as intuitively know the right sources to gain honest knowledge and wisdom from. For me, the greatest source of wisdom is the bible.

One of the most fascinating discoveries made known to me, is that we will all have challenges custom designed with exactly what we need to learn and walk through at that point in life we are facing. This is especially true when we fall out of alignment with our heart. At times it does not make sense, but trust that there is a reason for everything. There is divine order to everything and nothing is random.

Creation is fact and our life we experience takes direction from our thoughts, so retain only good thoughts and maintain good behavior. What science is just now realizing is that thoughts are energetic. There are interesting experiments related to the impact of your thoughts on water by Masaru Emoto. It is well worth researching as he has proven that the intention of our thoughts will impact the crystalline structure of water. What is awesome about this is that the effects can be physically seen in frozen water crystals under a microscope. This should in itself eliminate any doubt to the power of thought and intention. The difference between positive thoughts and negative thoughts are astonishing when looking at the test results and you can easily find them on the web by searching for him. There are even experiments on how thoughts impact plants. The Myth Busters did two excellent experiments on plants and thoughts and the results even surprised them. Thoughts were proven to impact the plants. You really should look into researching this topic more if you have any doubts. What you find will convince even the most skeptical person.

I want you to also understand that there are differences in a person's ability to influence their surroundings, people, places and things based upon how they think. The magnitude that the thought has on experiencing reality relates to the power and strength behind the thought. Remember too that emotions impact our thoughts. I also want to point out that if our energy flow is clogged or not functioning optimally due to carrying so much negativity and guilt, that will lessen the impact that your thoughts have on the surrounding reality you experience. Remember that you cannot lie to yourself and you always know deep down if you are telling the truth or not and how you are behaving. Truth is more powerful than lies and will have an effect on the power you have internally available. These are all variables that impact the abilities our thoughts have on everything around us.

I will try to explain the differences in the power of thought in terms of electricity and light, the more wattage you put into a light bulb the brighter it shines and the easier it is to see that reality. The better type of conduit utilized to carry the electricity from its source to its destination, the more energy reaches the destination. Bad conduit loses power on the way due to constrictions and is emitted as heat felt on the wiring. To further explain power, watts are defined as voltage multiplied by amperage. If our thoughts are defined as voltage and emotions is defined as the amperage used to describe how powerful they are, we can then think in these types of terms. The more we think about something the more voltage we energize into it and them more emotion we have behind those thoughts the more amperage we multiply it by. Therefore with a little emotion, you can energize the reality you want to experience. The third variable is the conduit and relates to how we transmit that thought energy in our field around us. As I mentioned, the conduit is the transfer method of the power from its source to its destination. If you have good conduit, nothing is lost in the transfer. If you have bad conduit, then power is lost on the way usually in the form of heat. For example, if you have faulty wiring in a house, things can short out or start a fire. This is similar to the flow of energy that surrounds your being. If your flow is clean and clear, not dirty and nothing is clogging it or inhibiting it and it is functioning at optimal levels then there is no energy loss when it is transmitted to your surroundings. The conduit relates to how pure, honest and blameless a person is. Someone who is free of bad energies is thought of as pure.

The factor of emotions is important as it determines the frequency utilized to emit the thought energy. Remember I said everything is energy and that light is a form of energy which we can see in the form of waves. When I discussed the 64 amino acid potential contact points with DNA, it is easy to understand the influence of the emotional state of the person in relation to the power of their thoughts. The bottom line is that emotions have a frequency, it oscillates and emits waves. EKG machines and MRI can be used to graph these waves.

Many songs talk in terms of love being a river, like a flow or current. It is not coincidence that these terms are used to describe love as they do a great job in explaining it. As I had previously mentioned, love operates at a higher frequency than fear. These are the two basic emotions that all other emotional derivatives stem from. Things like joy and happiness comes from love. Hate, anger, resentment, jealousy and many other negative feelings come from fear. Basically, all states of mind that nurture various emotional feelings are born from love or fear. This means, loving thoughts conquers all others when energized with the same voltage and amperage transmitted through good clean conduits. A clean body that is free of blockages or short circuits with pure honest loving emotions can emanate powerful thoughts. It is a perfect check and balance monitoring system. If you think about this, even if you have good thoughts and emotions, if you are dishonest and constantly accumulating sins, it will impede your energy flows and impact the reality you live in and your ability to influence it.

I again do not want to deviate too much on emotions and the base frequencies, but if you are interested in more research you will find a great deal of data on how we currently do measure output from the heart by reading electromagnetic radiation emanating from the heart. There are books and videos everywhere on that, and we use it in hospitals when we look at a person stress levels or how their heart is functioning by using an EKG machine. I also am not here to give you a lesson in electricity, but I do want you to know that electricity if used the wrong way can kill. Electricity if short circuiting can cause fires. Choose wisely and monitor what you are engaging in. Always pay attention to what you think. Pay special attention to emotions, especially those charged with bad or negative thoughts. Stay away from as much drama as possible. Drama just brews more negative energy and constricts the flow of good thoughts and good clean energy.

When dealing with emotionally charged situations, try to respond and not react. By definition, if you respond to a situation, then you are calmly thinking through the circumstance and you maintain control of your emotions. If you react to situations, then you are out of control and the emotions are acting for you. Think of it in these terms, when getting treatment from a doctor, the doctor wants the patient to respond well. The doctor does not want the patient to have a reaction, as a reaction is normally not good for the patient. Stay on top of what is making you emotional. Bad emotional feelings, brings up more negative feelings so try to steer clear of these circumstances. I want to make sure you understand that everything you do matters. Every word you say, every action you do, every thought you have. It all matters, I am not exaggerating as I am telling you the 100% truth. You have free will, use it wisely and choose who or what you surround yourself with.

In making decisions, choose the high road always. Keep on rising and do not let someone pull you down. Try not to over complicate a decision as you know what is right and wrong. When in doubt as to what you should do, rely on wisdom. One of my favorite expressions is "What would Jesus Do?" (WWJD), I love the bracelets I have seen kids wear with that abbreviation printed on them. I love all the positive energy in the form of t-shirts, posters and stickers that come from these simple but powerful words of wisdom. It is reminding us that if we are not sure whether we should do something, we can ask ourselves a very simple question "What would Jesus do?". If you act the way that you know in your heart that Jesus would act, then you will make the right choice. By choosing the same way Jesus would choose, you are basically choosing your will to be that of God's will for you. Remember that Jesus constantly prayed to our father in heaven and said to God, "your will not my will be done." This is very similar to turning your will and life over to the care and protection of God. Doing this is a way to trust in his guidance. This exact process is done in many programs designed to help people. When it seems like it did not work, it is always traceable to human error. If you choose to turn your will over, it must be done 100% of the time to work. Doing it part time or only when it suits you, does not work. Picking and choosing what to turn over and what to hang on to only leads to further frustration and a blame game that allows you to try and blame God for your failures. When anyone chooses to turn their life over, they must do it completely as anything else is just a recipe for failure. I have watched personally many people stumble on this. If you fail to take responsible action to act in accordance with God's principles, then it is inconceivable that you turned your will over. By then taking an honest look of your own actions if you see anything that would not coincide with the same decision that God would want then clearly you have not turned your will over 100% of the time.

Actions do speak louder than words. What I mean by that in relationship to identifying if you have truly turned your will over is to look at the actions and behaviors. Obvious behavior indicative of this failure to turning your will over can be clearly demonstrated by the actions someone takes. For example, when a person is using such nasty foul language, obscene vulgarities and is so wrapped up in drama that they never quite hear the message. No one can honestly think or say they turned their will over with such behavior. The answer is obvious and they know deep down and hopefully they work on it. Normally when this happens, the person is so self-absorbed and addicted to drama and control that they are unable to see that they have not turned their will over immediately, but if they slow down and look then the answer is obvious. The simple acid test by comparing the behavior to "what would Jesus do" or "what would Jesus say" is another clear revelation as whether their will has actually been turned over. What I mean by this is quite simple and I have stated it before. Keep it simple and don't over complicate decisions, actions and behaviors. When your will has been turned over to God, you will act and talk in the same manner as Jesus. Jesus would not be cursing and using foul language all over the place. We know this to be true. If ever you are not sure if you have turned over your will, just think about your actions and behavior and test it against what you know Jesus would have done.

I spent some extra time on this as I want you to always think about your actions and behaviors, even when you think no one is looking. The truth is, someone always is looking. That person is you and you cannot lie to yourself. You always honestly know if you are doing good or bad things and it will have an impact on the very reality in which you live. Be aware of how you are treating and talking to your peers, parents, teachers, friends, or anyone. Choose your words carefully and be kind always. If you have nothing nice to say, don't say anything. If you do choose to respond to someone who is being nasty and ugly to you, still respond in a forgiving and loving manner. Reacting to someone's behavior, actions or words in a bad way lets bad energy into your heart. I found confirmation of what I learned from various spiritual programs, even though I learned the hard way too. I recommend you read more and expand on it. You can find this truth in a passage from the bible where it is clearly stated.

Mathew 15:11 - ¹¹ it is not what goes into the mouth that defiles a person, but it is what comes out of the mouth that defiles a person.

Mathew 12:36-37 ³⁶ I tell you, on the day of judgment people will give account for every careless word they speak, ³⁷ for by your words you will be justified, and by your words you will be condemned."

What it I am saying here is be conscious of every word you say, eliminate the desire to speak with foul language or to speak harshly against others. There is no need to swear to get you point across, no need for all that drama and negative emotion. In the long run it is the person who spews vulgarities, lies or other nasty words that is defiled in the process. Chances are good that you will be tested in life in different ways. What I offer here is to stay true to your word. Remain calm and level headed and do not react cold hearted towards anyone. In time this becomes easier and easier to do. It is truly amazing how this happens as you eliminate negative energies from yourself. If those difficult times do arise, know that you are not alone and understand that God is with you. Know that I am also with you. This is a difficult concept to explain but I will try. The people we love and keep in our heart are always with us wherever we go. In time you will understand this even more. We are always connected and if you search hard enough you will feel how true that is. Lean on God and Jesus Christ when you need help, they are always there. Keep in your heart the principles in this book to guide you if you need help making the right choice. Prayer is always helpful, just stick around and listen for the response. Realize that the response may come in forms other than words. Be ready to receive what you asked for as God knows what you need before you even ask, but you must ask.

I consider myself a student of life always willing to learn more and a servant always willing to try and help. Know that as I gathered these details and organized them in this book, I am providing guidelines and not rules for you. I am not here to hinder your free will as you grow into an adult. I only want to gather my lessons from my life in a central place that you can utilize if you need a little help, think of this as you get older as "note comparing". Life is our teacher and we all are students. You can compare what I wrote to what you are experiencing and make your own judgment calls. Providing definite rules is not fair to you, as you must have free will to learn and grow and decide to do what is right on your own. Perhaps you can add to what I have learned, perhaps you may find somewhere it can be improved upon. I have no desire to take away your free will. Part of what we must learn in life is to use our free will to choose wisely as we navigate through life. I want to just share with you my experiences and what I have learned. In this way, if you so choose you can use these experiences as a guide to diminish any negative impact from any of your lessons. Each of us has to learn our own way and I am here for you and will always be. Some of us can make sense of guidelines or advice from others thereby having the ability to minimize the suffering that may be encountered in life. Others must experience it for themselves first hand, others a combination of firsthand experience and guidelines. I only wish to provide you a resource that you can look through if you want to and if you feel you need some guidance. For me, the hardest lesson was learning about who was telling the truth and who was telling lies. What I found out is that I had based many decisions and actions on lies. These lies were cleverly veiled in truth which was why it was so easy to believe. This same fictitious philosophy is universally present all around us and it is up to us to determine if it is true before we depend on it.

I am not perfect. I had to pay a great deal in the way of sin debt in order to learn firsthand what worked and what didn't. I was given ample advice and had access to good information even at an early age. Unfortunately I was also provided lies and confused. If you think about it, it is easy to have someone follow a lie. Tell them what they want to hear so that they will follow that false teaching or philosophy. I learned too that a person will judiciously defend a principle and concept even if it is not true so long as they receive a benefit from it. This is what makes a good person fall into the allure of money. People do outrageous things for money. People desire money cause it buys them prestige and materialistic things. These two things are dangerous. Money and prestige cultivates a supremacy false identity and materialism further disconnects us from what is truly real. Because of this, all through the ages money has been labeled as the root to all evil. If money is your master, then you will be led astray. That is a fact. This is depicted in the bible many times and I have a couple short passages that you can look at.

1 Timothy 6:10 For the love of money is a root of all kinds of evil: which some reaching after have been led astray from the faith, and have pierced themselves through with many sorrows.

Mather 6:24 [24] *"No one can serve two masters, for either he will hate the one and love the other, or he will be devoted to the one and despise the other. You cannot serve God and money.*

At the time I was completely unaware that I was measuring my success the wrong way. The definition of what was success meant was all wrong in my mind. I was baffled and confused from an early age. This basic concept is so easily mixed up. As I best can describe, this confusion was on purpose and orchestrated by very negative dark energies all around us. They do this throughout culture and societies everywhere. Few have understood how important is it to truly know the truth and live by the truth.

The few that understood, understood it so well that they gave up everything; they gave all their material possessions, their identity and their body in some cases. I want for you to have the gift of vision so that you will see the truth faster than I did. My eyes are beginning to focus, but it took some time. I am just now starting to truly live and accumulate real wealth, spiritual wealth. Chasing the illusion of happiness based on identity, physical pleasure and materialistic things will keep you away from seeing the truth. Keep an open mind and remember this information from time to time as you grow. Your learning and waking up process will be shortened so that you have the ability to live right from an early age. As you grow, embrace the pain and suffering as much as the happiness. Know that every experience has something to offer in the way of learning. Every mistake I did was exactly what I needed at the exact time I needed it. If I had been paying attention to this fact, I would have not made so many mistakes. Looking back now through the eyes of an observer, it is obvious to see the relationship links to experiences in life in proportion to how I was behaving or acting prior to the events in my life. As I have stated, I will share the hard lessons in life I learned with you when the time is right.

As I write this short version book, I am now 40 years old. I look back at the many times I missed the message life was trying to send me. What is beautiful about it now, is that I have no regrets. I accept that everything I experienced was related to my behaviors in some way. Those lessons taught me the truth. This in itself is important to realize, if I did not learn it the way I did I may not have learned it as well as I have. If I did not learn through the hard ways that I did, I may not have had the drive to write this book in a concise format for you. Understand that communication comes in many formats, not just language. Life does not speak with words, sometimes in actions or the peacefulness of the surroundings. Be aware that life speaks to us in many ways, and the way it speaks to you may be different than the way it speaks to me. Maybe life sends you certain feelings when listening to certain music, or maybe in your dreams you receive messages. It is best to slow down and listen to what life is trying to tell us, it will pay many dividends in the long run. Play the role of the observer in your own life when trying to listen to the messages life is sending you. Open the pages of your life's experience and look at what manifested in your reality. Look with honesty to find the underlying cause for the significant events in life. Everything is synchronized as nothing happens by coincidence. Know this to be true and appreciate the perfection in the design and the sheer magnitude and profound effect this knowledge will have on your life.

The lie that we are told and made to believe is that life just exists and we have no control, we just experience life. We are told that we are first born then later we die and that is the way it is. We are told that if things do not go right, we are stuck with the life we have and that life isn't fair. We are told that we are unable to do anything about it. That we are victims in life and it is our predetermined destiny. In extreme cases, we are told that nobody cares and you have to look out for yourself. We are told people do not care for each other. These lies suit many of us just fine, for if we realize the truth that we impact the life that we experience then we have to accept the fact that we are responsible for much of what we attract into our lives. That means there is order and balance to life, a cause and effect. I tell you that life is fair, extremely fair. You reap what you sow, so do not worry about the other person as they will reap what they sowed. Nobody gets away with anything, God will see to it. Let God worry about their injustice as he will deal out justice the way he wants to. Worry about your own actions. Remember that we have a choice to surround ourselves with like minded people that believe in the fundamental structure in that people do care and do love each other. Spread the truth to people, share with them what you have learned from life and this book.

We have a choice to not do the same things over and over. We have a choice to not do what our body wants, but to do what is right. The more we do what is right, the easier that becomes. When we want to change for the better, we should find people willing to love us and will help us by supporting us while we change and grow. This does means that sometimes, the people places and things you surrounded yourself with need to change. If the change is not something you can do permanently for some reason, then definitely you must temporarily. You need to make the change at least temporarily as you have to be strong in your changed belief to influence your surroundings. In order to be around those past influences, you need confidence and faith in your new behaviors. If you want to help the people still clinging onto the lies that we have been told, you need to be such a positive influence and you help wake them up so they can see and hear the truth. By your actions and behaviors, you send an important message. You can bring them up as opposed to them bringing you down as long as you are confident in your newly resurrected faith and beliefs.

There is a divine structure to life and any chaos we experience is directly related to our own actions and thoughts. There are many proofs attesting that our very thoughts impact the reality around us. Early in the discovery of the science that defines the understanding of the world inside of atoms, Einstein and Niels Bohr in the 1927 conference on quantum mechanics started a debate over some fascinating discoveries that seem to defy logic. It was what came to be known as the Copenhagen interpretation that Bohr had proposed which had started the debate. These set of equations described characteristics where entities, like electrons could be considered real, but at the same time, the entities didn't actually exist as particles until someone were looking for them. What was more perplexing is the notion where probabilities come in to describe the location of the electron in relationship to its speed. This is what is known as the uncertainty principle. The logic appalled Einstein so much, that he made this statement many times "God does not play dice with the universe". What is intriguing is that once you comprehend the magnitude of the discoveries, you can realize that they were both right. The world of the small can be described as probabilities in a way and it is by design so as to not impede our free will. Through reading our energy levels, the probabilities of future events to be experienced can be ascertained which then clearly identifies another anomaly. The difficult concept where everything that can happen has already happened and that we can change future events by changing our thoughts is also both true. If you take the time to study this area of science, you will understand how this is validating the very nature of sacred passages in religion that were cleverly cloaked until a time that we would be able to understand them.

The famous quantum physics test conducted that proves the idea that our thoughts impact the very reality in which we live is the double slit experiment. Do some research and watch some videos on this. It explains at a high level that the observer has a role into what possible outcome they will experience based upon simply observing. It is then the belief system in which the observer accepts that is sending thoughts in the form of energy as wave functions. These wave functions tell the electrons how to act through attraction. Through this force of attraction by which the most powerful thought based upon conviction and emotion prevails.

Other proven tested experiments are the random number generators that under certain conditions no longer provide random numbers. More of these anomalies were discovered during highly emotionally triggered events around the world. If we look at the events from the world trade centers and the random number generators, it is remarkable how the numbers defied randomness. When we think of this in forms of vibrations, we can then apply a new meaning to the great symphony of life and how the combination of such vibrating waves of energies, through the combined efforts of our thoughts holds frequencies in place providing for the reality we experience at various collective levels of consciousness. Again, I do not want to get too far off topic. Just know that there is a wealth of information, books and videos that validate the fact that the world in which we live is interactive by way of proof through quantum physics for anyone seeking the proof.

We can impact the reality around us with our thoughts, in other words the world is very much alive and we can make it grow around us in different ways. In philosophical terms, if we were all in an orchestra playing a musical instrument we would create a sound. If everyone we surrounded ourselves with was of good heart and mind, the harmony being played would be so beautiful that we would not want to stop hearing it. If there were some lousy musicians making horrible sounds at the same time we would not experience the true harmony that we were supposed to experience. This should give you a new perspective on who you want to surround yourself with, as well as whether your behavior is one that a perfect orchestra would want you to be a part of. I love this expression, "Is my attitude worth catching?". Think about that as you interact with people throughout the day. Be the positive influence, bring those around you up and do not let them bring you down. If you feel yourself being brought down, leave the circumstance with that person, place or thing.

One of the issues we face as a society and individually is the inability to recognize how our actions influence life. It may be obvious to an observer, but not to someone who is a part of the total experience. As I was a part of the experience and did not know I was influencing the very experience life was presenting me, it was hard to be truly objective. Each time something I did not like happened to me I only wanted to get out of that situation. I never was concerned about what the root cause was. It took me a long time to figure out that part. I was so wrapped up in materialism and ego, and it is ego that prevents and blocks the truth from penetrating into your heart and mind so you can do something about it. The ego does everything it can to protect the current belief system even if the belief system does not work. We cling to these false beliefs and old ideas and sometimes we take them to the grave. That is the illusion we all must realize exists and we must accept that we may be wrong in what we believed all our lives. We have to realize that sometimes we chase something that is not real, thinking it is real. We let ourselves be fooled into believing that happiness is based upon getting something materialistic or some physical pleasure. We sometimes even fool ourselves into believing the wrong philosophy just to be right, as the ego never likes to be wrong.

The ego would rather make us feel right and accept the wrong philosophy than to admit it was wrong to begin with. We chase this illusion of the importance of material wealth and layers of identities in the form of an ego, or as the bible put it; the desires of flesh. Some wealthy company leaders know this and sometimes use questionable philosophies to further fatten their wallets. I have known them to place a goal just outside the reach of the employee in order to keep the employee on the hamster wheel chasing a goal they may never get. The management is taught this philosophy in training classes and they are told it is for employee morale, to keep the employee focused on the goal working harder. The management then believes what they are doing is right, they do not know they are under the influence of negative energy.

They also tend to cultivate a culture where ego and identities fester and grow as everyone competes with each other for a position with more money or prestige. They further add to the identification and ego issue through recognition programs by using them in the wrong way. Some of these companies are not offering a true thank you or real appreciation for the work. If that was the goal of these programs, than that is all that would be needed by the employees. In fact, rather than the management themselves nominating their employees, they depend heavily on fellow employees to nominate someone. If they were paying attention, the management themselves would just know who deserves extra appreciation as it is clearly evident to see someone work who truly loves what they do and is willing to put extra effort in.

Recognition programs are easy for corporations to justify as it is cheaper to offer recognition awards than to do the right thing and offer decent salary increases that at a minimum match the cost of living increases over time. Another common practice by company leaders under the influence of negative energy is to shift costs to the employees. They reduce or eliminate things like bonuses or reimbursements amounts. In some cases they eliminate the benefit completely. The most common practice is to adjust health insurance amounts. Health insurance increases are passed directly to the employee and the benefits offered under these plans are reduced. I was dismayed when I found all these practices to be true of many management philosophies. The management sell themselves on the idea that people will work harder for fulfillment of identity rather than a fair days' wage. As they internally breed the importance of employee recognition, they are further adding to the need to be divided and for some to feel supremacy. Doing all this only further propagates the lie that recognition is what the employees want. As one corporation adopts this practice, others follow behind. They then sell the concept to their employees that they are within industry standards. Do not be fooled by them. Do not let the lure of goals tied to money or materialistic gains they never plan to fulfill cloud your vision. Stay away from the fascination with identity that is contained within recognition programs blind you from seeing what are truly right and wrong. Do a fair days' work for a fair days' pay. Do it in a field that you love. Do not take a position in a field that will add separation to your true self by growing the ego.

If you do what you love, then it does not even feel like working and the salary always feels like a bonus. The management that buys into the philosophy of using recognition programs over salary increases is doing so because that philosophy is exactly what they want to hear. It makes them wealthier through bonuses as they save money on salaries since the employee is now working for recognition in order to build their ego and identity. Look for a truly honest company where the income disparity for the workload and work is negligible and where they offer a sincere thank you. If you are not at a good place now, you must still work and fulfill your obligation to meet the job requirements. Remember, there is no need to judge them harshly or act out against the company by being a bad employee, God will take care of them in the long run. While you continue working there, take the time to find something else as you will be much happier in the long run. Remember, you want to surround yourself with positive energy. Eventually if everyone looks for this type of workplace, the greedy negative companies will have nobody to work for them.

Stay aware of the trickery in many businesses and how they manipulate the system on purpose. You will know the difference as soon as you start working. You will see the different characteristics between a greed oriented company and a company that truly cares about their employees. All companies boast that they care about their employees, but as always use the acid test and ask yourself things like, WWJD if he was running the company? An even simpler comparison is if the management would like adhering to the same policy they are having you adhere to. For example, in relation to the recognition program think about whether the senior managers adopting the recognition philosophy would themselves prefer employee of the month as opposed to a fair wage or bonus. Sounds silly now that you think of it in these terms, but many are fooled by the lie. Let us be honest, I do not know of a grocery store, daycare or gas station that accepts my employee of the month awards as payment for food, services or gas. If the managers truly believed this philosophy and they just wanted recognition, then they could give up their yearly bonus and salary and give it to their employees. They surely would receive much praise and recognition for doing such a wonderful selfless deed. Let's face the facts; these senior managers are stuck in greed, materialism, money and ego. If ever you lead a company, please remember to treat everyone fairly and that means fair wages for a fair days work. I pray that the company leaders and management see their error, for they are fooling themselves into believing their behavior is right and just. What they fail to see is that they will be judged in the end. If they do not recognize their error, God will see to it in some way. The way God takes care of it and balances the effects is not for us to determine. There is no need to waste time worrying about how that will occur. Maybe God will allow calamities to materialize in their life in an attempt to try and wake them up before it is too late but again, that is up to God. Here is a passage from the bible on this topic.

Mathew 19:24 [24] *Again I tell you, it is easier for a camel to go through the eye of a needle than for a rich person to enter the kingdom of God."*

It is a cycle that many fall into, some of us worse than others. Once we realize how we are letting ourselves be fooled and we open our eyes, we can stop it. Realizing this gives us the power to look at the situation from a much higher perspective so that we can intentionally make the choice to not listen to our ego if it is going to lead us into a problem or lead us nowhere. We will be able to choose what is truly in our best interest even if that means a change in our environment, like a job or career. By sleeping at the wheel of my body and letting my ego drive my decisions, I had spent much of my life constantly putting the fires out. I never looked to see how the fires were started each time. As I was not paying attention, the fires grew larger and larger. Life was trying to tell me to change, but I did not listen. Life also knows that pain is a great motivator when all else fails in getting my attention. It starts out with little growing pains, but as time went on since I was deaf to the noise and ignored the pain, it grew in intensity. I was not living true to myself and building up layers of protection in the process. I was hiding behind this false identity called the ego. By living this lie, my true self was trying to get my attention by causing calamities to manifest in my life. I made things worse by further covering my true self up and hiding the emotional pain I was going through with more layers of identity as I was not living in harmony with my true self. I fell into the trap that most of us do. I wrongly believed that we must accumulate as much material things as we can. I fell into the belief that no one can know our true self, for if they knew they may not like what they see. The fact is that if you are true to yourself and you display your true self, if someone does not like you then most likely they are not living true to themselves. If we think about this carefully and evaluate it for its own merits, who would not want to be around an honest, good natured person who surrounds himself with good things and light? The answer is obvious; someone not honest, a bad seed who lives in darkness will stay away. In the bible this too is talked about.

John 3:20 - ²⁰ For everyone who does wicked things hates the light and does not come to the light, lest his works should be exposed.

This truth took me a little bit to understand. I realized that as I was changing, my connection to old friends was disappearing and new ones were appearing. It just happens that way, the cleaner you become the less likely you will attract people around you that are dirty, for they do not want others to see the dirt they have accumulated. I hope that you can remain clean and pray that you can avoid the avalanche of material illusion and clearly see through it early in life. The three principle concepts on how to live will help you to live truthful and remain that way at a much younger age than I. It will also help eliminate the need to go through all the heartache. Simply by your good actions you can help those around you without even saying a word, but you will be qualified to speak if the need arises. These three principle concepts are not new, but many overlook the importance of them. Many do not realize that by not using them, they can avoid much pain. Many do not know that there is a simple solution to eliminating the debt we incur in guilt from the sins we have committed and therefore I want you to know this process well.

It is important to understand, that you can be free and therefore do anything you believe in. The less debt you have, the more freedom you experience. The more freedom you have, the easier it is to do what you intend to do. All you have to do is ask for it in prayer and believe. I do not say this metaphorically, I say it literally. Here is a passage from the bible that details this in Mark 11:24-25:

²⁴ Therefore I say to you, whatever you pray and ask for, believe that you will receive it, and it will be so for you. ²⁵ And whenever you stand up to pray, if you have something against anyone, forgive so that your Father in heaven may forgive you your wrongdoings.

The requirement is simple. In order to accomplish great things with less effort you need to not carry a lot of weight in wrongdoings. You want to be free of the debt of sin and not a slave to sin. In order to be free, you must do what is right always and be forgiven for anything you fell short of being good, as well as forgive all others. You want to be as virtuous, honest and blameless as a person as you can be. If you fail or fall short, correct it quickly and ask for forgiveness. Remember in order to be forgiven you must also forgive everyone who has trespassed, sinned or incurred a debt against you. Once you are free, do not incur new sin debt. Remember early on I mentioned that accumulation of bad energy leads to constrictions to the flow of energy in your body, it ruins the conduit and these constrictions to the energetic flows of energy can manifest as physical health problems. This is very key in understanding the true consequences of not following the three principles. By not doing what is good, you hurt the very abilities and the power emanating from your thoughts. I found this important message in the bible on the power of prayer from a righteous person.

James 5:16 -[16] *For this reason, confess your sins to each other and pray for each other so that you may be healed. The prayer of the righteous person is powerful in what it can achieve.*

This passage is clearly showing us that if we are true, honest and blameless we in essence would be able to achieve great things. Our spiritual being would not be sick or dying, it would be truly alive and you would be living. If we had no debt in the forms of sins, we would be completely healed. Relating this to the energy flows in our body, we then would have full power released when we prayed and asked for something from our father in heaven. A righteous, honest and blameless person would not ask for bad things, he would ask for good things. A righteous person would not be seeking things to build false identities or in materialistic things to seek happiness. This is important to know and understand. We will definitely be coming back to this and expand upon in the principles.

Suffering and the ego

I mentioned this earlier, but will mention this again. Pain is a great motivator, for when I was in severe pain I could drop to my knees and pray without thinking; it was almost instinctively. Whenever I experienced heartache and calamities I did pray and the intensity of my prayer always seemed to be related to the intensity of the situation I landed myself into. At times, the situations I was in seemed to be unfair and undeserved. In retrospect, every occurrence was exactly what I needed and a very necessary part of my life. The situations always seemed to grow with intensity, like someone was knocking on the door louder and louder trying to get me to hear them. Somehow I made it through all the situations so I just continued on with life. Eventually there would be that one knock on my door that was so loud, that I would have no choice but to hear it. That knock came for me and I did wake up. The knock never has to get as loud or difficult as it did for me. I call these situations growing pains now, but when I went through them I did not see the growth in them at all. I went through various emotional stages each time. This eventually made me realize how spiritually bankrupt I had become. In truth, I did not see it that way right away. This was the beginning to what I call soul searching. Eventually it led to the admission that I was the one common variable in all the situations. Of course, even with that realization I still had idea that it was everyone else's fault in some strange way. I thought life was punishing me, that life was out to get me and everyone I knew was in on this big secret. I felt like a victim, my life was always filled with drama. Over and over I kept digging trying to make sense of all the chaos. As I approached an answer, things always seemed harder and it just got worse. What I did not realize is that there were forces surrounding me trying to prevent me from seeing the truth as to how things worked, for if I understood the truth I would then know how to live debt free and truly live.

I was being tested and I was given lessons all at the same time. You must know that in life the tests are necessary. Each one of us will have perfectly designed tests that we must walk through to get to the next stage in life. One reason for the test may be to "Weed" out those not worthy yet, or those who are doing things for the wrong reason. You see, if you have faith and you trust and believe in the right principles you will keep on going regardless of how the situation looks, you don't give up. You know what you are doing is right and true so that keeps you going regardless of what falls in your way. Understand that God does not give you more than you can handle, even if it looks that way. Below is a passage from the bible on this exact topic.

1 Corinthians 10:13 ¹³ No temptation has overtaken you that is not common to man. God is faithful, and he will not let you be tempted beyond your ability, but with the temptation he will also provide the way of escape, that you may be able to endure it.

The testing of my faith was absolutely necessary for me to understand and to realize something very critical, that it is impossible to hide the truth from yourself. No matter how hard you want to justify and rationalize why you do things the way you do, you can never lie to your true inner self. You can lie, perhaps consciously to others as to reasons why you want to be a good person or honest, but you can't lie to yourself. In other words, if the reason you want to be good is so you can get things or do great things and not because it is the right thing to do then you will be stuck as you are indeed being dishonest. To be honest, blameless and a truly righteous person, you do the right thing always. You do the right thing with no expectation of gaining materialistic things. You simply do the right thing because it is the right thing to do and if you do fall short, you take corrective action as soon as you realize it so as to not incur sin debt.

For me, the truth of the core causation for the experience I was being tested against was far stranger than I ever imagined. The knowledge learned I do not think I could ever have gained without the suffering I experienced as well as the faith I had available to me. I was lucky in that I did have faith, even if I questioned my faith, it was still enough to hold me up when I leaned on it. In time, I began to trust my faith and lean on it more and more, realizing it was sturdier that I had thought. This is what in fact eventually led me to change my ways. I was not a blameless, honest or righteous person by any stretch of the imagination. Looking back at myself, if you really knew me, I was not the person most people would want to have as a friend. I did try to find shortcuts and sometimes that entailed "white lies", which is another lie we tell ourselves to justify lying. There is just lying, not white lies or non-white lies. I always looked for the easy way out. It was a bit of laziness and dishonesty neatly wrapped up in my ego. I did sin and I did carry a lot of weight in sin debt most of my life which is why these challenging situations always seemed to manifest in my life. What I want for you to realize in your younger years is that you can avoid all this turmoil and in so doing, you will truly live. Even if you don't get the lesson early in life, it is never too late and you can still make a change.

What I want to make clear is that it does not matter the intensity of the situation that life throws at you. The situations always start out small and the situations grow until it gets your attention. Perhaps you currently have a simple situation where you are assigned to a project with fellow classmates in school and one of your fellow classmates is not pulling their weight. That classmate who is not doing their fair share of the work will have their own issue to deal with later. Do not focus on what they are not doing, worry about yourself. This is a trick of the ego, to have you look at the faults of others to justify acting out or justify your bad behavior. Be the leader and do what is right. Evaluate and just know that in order to still get a good grade, you and the other team members have to do extra work to make up for what someone is not doing. If you do the right thing and just do the extra work, you will see that in actuality the classmate not putting forth the effort does not gain anything. Remember I said that no one gets away with anything, we are each our own internal record keepers. The classmate falling short in their contribution to the project actually has committed a trespass against you and other team members (if others exist). Know the truth, that by you leading the way and doing the right thing in doing the extra work for the better grade, you actually will gain spiritual gifts by acting virtuous. As you gain enough of these spiritual gifts, it just seems that life becomes easier for you. Synchronization of life is in perfect harmony. These experiences of synchronicity can manifest in simple ways, like always having a good day of fishing every time you go or always getting a close parking spot at the grocery store.

I do not want to drift too far into what one will gain and what one will lose based upon their behavior. I just wanted to give you a quick simple example that you can relate to now. Remember, it is not about the materialistic gains in life that man should use to validate their self worth. That is the illusion whereby the blind person who cannot see beyond the material world will gauge their self worth by. That scale is wrong, dead wrong and I mean that literally. Chasing that illusion is the great trap people fall into. They grow their vanity, identity and ego to the point that they forget who they truly are. One's value is based upon living and in order to live one must have spiritual wealth. Spiritual wealth comes from following the right principles in life. There is no other way gain it. Spiritual wealth is not for sale, you cannot buy your way into heaven. One who dies with the most toys does not win anything, most likely along the way he lost his soul as he traded it out for identity and the material things.

The truth is that each of us in life will experience suffering when we are drifting away from our purpose, it just happens. We are no longer in harmony therefore synchronicity of life events does not appear to be in line with what we want. The degree to which we experience the suffering is directly proportional to the good or bad deeds we have done in life and the layers of fake identity we have covering ourselves in the form of an ego. In different spiritual programs they label these experiences as fortune of luck, karma, sins or guilt. When we talk about these experiences, I want to be perfectly clear that there is no randomness in the way of luck, karma, good fortune or great experiences. What we experience is created by us directly bound by the good or bad ways in which we behaved to each other and ourselves. The energy field around us lights up and is fully charged when we behave in a good manner and we add to the energy by charging it for every good deed we do. At the same time, it goes dim as we behave in bad ways as we slowly drain the energy from our own energy field thereby making it harder and harder to create situations we want to experience as there is no energy to make it materialize. As you continue the journey into understanding, the analogy and facts will become apparent. I will try to explain this in more detail without making it too lengthy. My hope is that making it short and to the point, it will make sense to you and you will be motivated to research more of this on your own. I promise you, I would not tell you a lie as I only want to explain to you the truth that I have experienced firsthand and the source that has been around for years that tells us these very facts and in much more detail. It even provides examples once you understand what is written as the wisdom is cleverly veiled. I am just providing what is necessary to open your eyes in the hope that you will continue unveiling to yourself what is written.

When we understand the purpose of the suffering we are facing and realize the hidden message in it, we have the power to change ourselves for the better. We only need to learn to accept one of the hardest truths in life, that in some way we created that situation by some action or behavior in the past whether we remember it or not. Know that this is an opportunity to learn and a chance to embrace the pain and suffering so we can look deeper into ourselves to find where we can improve ourselves. The reason we are experiencing this pain is always made known to us if we honestly look hard enough. The hardest part to all this is the acceptance step, that we are responsible in some way. I want you to know this to be true. It took me a long time to see that fact. My ego did the job it was designed to do, to protect my beliefs and by doing so it prevented me from seeing this truth. When you are going through any pain in life you too can realize that even though you may not see it at that exact time, there is a reason for the pain. Life is trying to send you a message. It may be time to stop and listen. Know that if you are not ready to listen and accept this truth, life is patient and will try to reach out to you again. Each time it calls on you to listen, it gets louder as it has to break through more layers of the ego.

We must first thoroughly understand what an ego is. I have mentioned it is the flesh described in the bible and the identity we assign ourselves based upon experiences we live in. Identity does have a purpose, but when it grows to such a level that we forget who we truly are, it is dangerous. The first identity I associated myself with was a sound that was repeated to me over and over as an infant. Eventually I figured out through sound association that when that particular sound was made, it was for the purpose obtaining my attention. During this early stage of my development, my only role that I could play was that of a baby who knew nothing and needed to be taught everything. I was introduced to more sounds, smells and tastes. I was an observer, trying to learn how this thing called life worked. As I grew a little older, I came to realize that the sound directed towards me was in fact my name. This is the same process used on you. We pass along from generation to generation the need for identity. It was the first identity I associated myself with. What that meant, I clearly did not really know as I was just a baby. All I knew was when that sound was made someone was trying to get my attention. I am not unique to the experience of associating a sound to who we are. We all have gone through this first basic step in identification. We do this instinctively, with no thought or voice in our head telling us to do this. Somehow we just do this association of self with that given sound our parents gave to us. It is remarkable that as soon as we are brought into this world, one of the very first tasks we complete is learning who we are with no recollection of doing this. It is just natural that we as humans go from just "Being" to an identity made up of a sound.

At the same time as we learned our name, sound repetition was given to other objects that identified things, like who our parents were. Repeating the identifying sounds various words make, like mama and papa eventually we associate them to something like in this case, our parents. This is all innocent enough, but as we continue with the identification stage in life the identification need seems to manifest and continue to grow out of pressure to be something or someone we are not. I did not realize the importance of not trying to assign a label to anyone, but when I realized my error I began minimizing the degree that which I used labels around everyone.

One thing we must all recognize and be willing to accept is that we all have an ego, the beauty is that the ego is not who we are. When we realize this, we are on our way to waking up. That statement is powerful; it is a part of the energy that frees us to do anything. We are not confounded to the labels we are assigned in life. We are free to be who we want to be. We all have that ability to choose and create our own life as long as we are free.

Let us dissect the word ego and see how it relates to our everyday lives. We are all raised by someone who takes on the role as our parents. Parents have nothing but good intentions for you, the same as my parents did for me. Somewhere along the way in the attempt to teach me right from wrong and teach me what I needed to know, the illusion of the importance of the identity crept in. As we get older and we pass along lessons, I realized how important it is to correct this. Unknowingly I passed along much of the same lessons. The illusion of the importance of the identity crept in to my life and maybe you too. It just happens that way. If we learn the wrong lesson and never realize the error in it, we will pass it along and lean on the wrong belief system. Parents want us all to be unique and have an identity as my parents did for me. It makes perfect sense on the surface, especially if that is what we are all taught by our parents. We learn that lesson about being unique and having an identity very well. We eventually grow into a "role" of identifying with something. Sometimes this identity we relate ourself to has positive attributes; we are smart, good looking and maybe a good boy or good girl. Other times this identity has negative attributes; I am stupid, ugly, fat, brat, immature or maybe a bad boy or bad girl.

The intentions are usually good but sometimes no matter how good the intentions are, they have consequences. There is a danger in not realizing the truth in this concept that we are not the identity assigned to our physical bodies. I want to make it clear, that the ego or identity we create can be harmful if it takes over control of our lives. If we wrap ourselves up into falsifying our true nature, we can never be true to who we are. Society today is heading down a slippery road. With the invention of social media enterprises it has become so easy to add additional layers of fake identities to ourselves thereby letting the ego grow. I do not want to bash methods that can also be utilized to share love with each other, but when it is clearly evident that many people utilize these mediums as ways of falsifying who they really are, I want you to be aware so that you will stay away from the trap. We are truly energetic spiritual beings who manifest and experience life in this physical realm. The experiences we have are directly proportional to how well we stay away from negative behaviors and negative influences. We as parents unknowingly keep passing along the same errors in the importance of identity and ego, doing the same thing over and over. Einstein defined doing the same thing over and over and expecting different results as insanity. Try to stay sane and stop this vicious cycle of the illusion that labels, identity, materialism and ego are more important just being.

These labels will continue to haunt us as long as we continue to use them. The implications of the labels that create the illusion of the identity to the ego will not just impact our well being emotionally, or physically, but our very health. For instance, identifying with being fat by someone telling you that you are fat will surely lead to physically being fat. This label of "Fat" attaches to our ego so tight as to not let go once we accept it as true, even if it is a lie. The unconscious fear from the ego of losing identity, good or bad identity is the glue that binds the thought of the illusion of who we pretend to be. Here I introduce thought into how important it is in our daily lives. The thought is centered in the mind, but our ego and spirit both use this medium to communicate within our true selves. The skill needed to change our outlook in life is the ability to let our spirit be free and think in the right manner. Some call this turning ourselves or our will over to God, others call this spiritual enlightenment and others call this waking up. I believe it is the beginning to experiencing true freedom and that all three perspectives lead to the same revelation.

Knowing who I truly am was important in understanding why I was suffering over and over again. In order to do this, I had to let go of the ego if even for a short time to gain a new perspective. I had to ask the hard questions, like "Why did I always seem to fall into such situations that created immense pain for me emotionally and for those around me?" I know that things could have been easier for my kids growing up. I am sorry for causing unnecessary heartache to them and for the mistakes I made. I ask them to forgive me and my ignorance. I made many mistakes to many people and I only ask for their forgiveness as I just did not know. This is another reason why I felt it was important to share and write this book, so others can also realize the truth and be free. Realizing that I am not the labels I had been assigned in life or labels I assigned to myself was such a release. I could not have pierced through the protective layer of the ego myself, though. It indeed required a degree of suffering to take place to get through to my core self. If you follow the principles laid out, you will be able to minimize the degree of suffering you may face in life. This does not mean that in life we are guaranteed to not suffer. Sometimes we are given suffering just as a test of our faith and we cannot attribute past behavior to what we are facing. Stay faithful and true to yourself. Remain honest, blameless and righteous in order to pass through the test quickly. A quote by Winston Churchill; "If you're going through heck, keep going" (paraphrased). This is similar to walking on hot coals, keep walking and don't stop or you might get burned. Get through as quickly as possible, don't look back and don't create bad situations while you are going through it. Each successive run through becomes easier as you build up the confidence.

My suffering was emotionally intense. I was hard headed and had a very strong ego. That ego was very hard to penetrate. Know that it does not need to be that way. When you learn to listen to the messages in life and you face up to and accept the pain and suffering by finally working through it all, it will become your greatest triumph. This realization activates something in your very being that adds the strength to face each succeeding situation easier and quicker and provide you with a new perspective that will eventually lead into the elimination of suffering altogether. In other words, you will develop and learn the skills on how to suffer so you can navigate through any suffering with less pain each successive time.

As I expand the definition and further provide a clearer picture on the reasons for pain and suffering, keep an open mind. I know that nobody while in the crutches of suffering relishes and enjoy the pain at that time. Nevertheless suffering does have multiple functions or purposes. Suffering's obvious purpose is the ability it has to wipe away the superficial front we try to portray to each other. Many self help or counseling programs say something similar; before someone can recover they have to fall hard. What they know is that in order to improve their life, in order to heal themselves or recover, the individuals have to lose their tough false front they have built up over the years. This fake front is the ego that has been mentioned already. It is the same identity we talked about, it is the identity created through the association of labeling ourselves or others. The ego is a function of the identity attributed to the physical body.

The ego tries very hard to protect its own belief systems for in losing those beliefs it loses its own power over you. This is why it is so hard to communicate the truth to people as to how life works. It is the reason why it was so hard for me to see it. As long as I looked at the situation through the eyes of any identity attributed to who I was, my ego blocked my sight as the experience was filtered through the natural desire we all have to avoid pain and seek pleasure. The only way to experience this revelation is to see yourself through the eyes of the ultimate observer, one with no preconceived ideas or ideologies, no identity or image of himself or herself. The only way to do this is to remove yourself from all identification systems, materialisms or influences and just observe your life with no judgment. This is not an easy thing to do as we sometimes can get this view momentarily, but holding that view is key, and the longer we can hold it the more we see the truth.

Alternative terminology for the ego that is expressed in various literatures and sacred writings include terms like the garment we wear to cover up our true selves, a cocoon that we live in. It is this false identity we try to portray to everyone around us that keeps us from hearing the truth. As a garment, we expose it to the elements around us and it gets dirty. When we do not clean it, it can impact our daily attitudes as we carry around all this negative energy. If we are wrapped in a cocoon we can grow and fly away like a butterfly, but if we fail to grow we die inside the cocoon and are eaten by other organisms as we decay and rot away.

Another way we can incorrectly interpret who we are is the belief that we are only a physical body. Believing that we are only flesh and bones and nothing else is an illusion. That lie is a part of the attachment problem we all face with the ego. We unknowingly cling to our surrounding as we are trying to know who we are. The ego's identity assigned to ourselves breeds an attachment to the materialistic world and that attachment is just as dangerous to our true being as bad deeds. This misinterpretation of thinking of us as only flesh and bones is missing a critical component, our true self which is a spiritual being that has a soul. Regardless of the language used to describe the identity we use to cover our true nature, when we are suffering we begin to lose that false front. When we realize the truth of this statement, we can embrace and appreciate what suffering can do for us. In essence suffering is designed to erode or eliminate the ego's presence so that messages with truth can pierce the lies we have wrapped ourselves up in. This is stated by many wise people throughout the ages in many different ways.

Think about this, logically if you can learn and grow through pain and suffering, then good can come of it. Suffering by design has the ability to penetrate into our very soul so there is a reason for suffering and never forget that. Even if the suffering seems to defy logic in the case of a test, by perseverance we can still grow. We may not like it when we are in the middle of suffering, although if there is a positive that grows from it then there is a valid purpose for it whether we like it or not. As you get older, you may have to punish your children as I have had to punish mine when they were out of line. In essence, I in relation to my kids, I was wiping away the attitude that was growing from the identity they started to create for them self. When that happened to me, I felt like I was suffering and did not fully understand why I had to be punished and suffer at the time. As we grow older, we realize that it was necessary and we indeed grew from it. I also understand fully that one of the last things we want someone to say to us is that somehow we are responsible for the suffering we are experiencing. Please know that I am not trying to kick you in the teeth if you are suffering right now. I only want you to wake up and take charge of your life by knowing that you have the ability to change and the tools at your hands to create the very life you want. I want you to create your life the way you want to live it, not live a life that someone else has control over or a life someone else wants you to have. You have the right to live your life the way you see fit, but live it to your true self by knowing your true self. Depending how far you have fallen will directly relate to the time it can take to realize the changes in your life, of course faith and belief can greatly reduce the time required to reap the benefits from changing.

The realization delay

There is a simple fact in how it takes a while to reap the benefits of what we plant and nurture. It does not matter if we planted good or bad things. It takes a while to see the results. On top of that, the way in which we live feels like we are missing the instruction manual to life and learning through trial and error. The funny thing is that there is an instruction manual, it is the bible. Some of us choose not to read it or take a long time before we do. It is hard to determine what works if we do not understand how life works and if the results from our work take time to manifest in our reality it makes it even harder to match up our effort with the results. Add one more variable, how well in sync we are with life. When we are not synchronized to how we are living, it is even more difficult to judge what is happening. By not living life true ourselves, creating the very things in life we want to experience does not seem as though we are impacting the creation of the reality we experience at all. Simple incidents in life play out in ways that create frustrating events further adding to drama that echoes the negative feelings we have buried deep within ourselves. We have to understand that the ability to realize exactly what we create in our thoughts quickly is directly proportional to how clean our energy flow is in our body and the power and energy behind that thought. If we are living the right way and we have no debt that causes energy blockages, then realizing our reality just happens at a much faster rate. It can be as fast as our thought reaches our heart and we set it free in some cases. There is a logical reason for this. Faith and belief is required. It is called the mystery of faith in many religions for a purpose. We are so submersed in a lifestyle where "Seeing is believing" that we lose sight of wisdom passed down in various teachings. In actuality it works the other way, "Believing is seeing". You have to believe in something in order to attract a specific experience into your reality. The more you believe in it, the more likely you just do it without consciously even thinking about it. You just do it, as you are so confident subconsciously in the actions you take. Believing and acting as though you have already received it will make it appear in your experience of reality. Stay away from those who have little faith and do not believe, for they will poison your true beliefs. Again I will refer to the bible for a passage that clearly demonstrates this.

Mark 11:24 *[24]Therefore I tell you, whatever you ask in prayer, believe that you have received it, and it will be yours.*

Why this is so difficult to accept is that our belief system has been infiltrated and corrupted so much that we have lost the importance of trusting in faith and believing in truth. We see movies or we hear slogans with messages that say things like "Show me the money" or "Greed is good" that we end up letting ourselves get confused with what is right. We want immediate satisfaction by way of manifestation of things to appear in our reality in order to believe, but I tell you that will not occur if you are living in sin. Realizing it is sin that is keeping you from seeing the fruit of your works is a blessing. Realizing the results of your behaviors and activities is not as simple as touching a hot stove, whereby immediately you retract your hands as you feel the burn. You must first believe and believe in what is true. Believe what is written in the bible, it has great knowledge. The realization of many good things or bad things when you sin is on a delay on purpose, the less you believe or the more sins you have, the longer the delay.

As I mentioned earlier, the delay works in a similar way as knowing that smoking is not good for you. Realizing that it causes health problems and can eventually lead to death takes time. Your body is accumulating the negative effects of smoking. When it does manifest the effects, sometimes it is too late to reverse all the damage. Even knowing that smoking is not good for you does not keep everyone from participating. They will rationalize and justify that they are the exception to the rule and not be impacted as badly as other smokers. They also will say that they are only smoking temporarily and will quit soon. I understand that much of what I discuss and show you takes time to realize, but it is worth it in the long run.

As you act with good virtuous behaviors with the right intentions, the quality of life improves and you do better overall in many ways. In addition to what we achieve in our daily living and the benefits in the physical world there also spiritual gifts we will receive. I carefully qualify the words "right intentions". For example, if you do something good like return a wallet you found only because you wanted a reward and not because it was the right thing to do, then the right intention was missing in your good deed. If you encounter someone who wants to see the gains first before they do things right, they would not be doing things the right way on the basis of merit. Steer clear of these types of people, for they will poison your energy and corrupt your thoughts. Doing things because it is right and solely because it is the right thing to do is the best way to be righteous in your actions. I do understand that much of what I want you to see and believe in as well as the sources of some of the knowledge requires faith. Search your heart to know that I will not knowingly lie to you or lead you away from the truth as I want you to live in the light.

The side effect that happens in life as we become more and more enslaved with identities and materialism is we get dependent on the very things that are causing us to get sick. We get addicted in a way to it for we lose our self control over it. In order to evaluate if you are on the right path, you need to take a break from the life you are living. You need to slow down. In a way you need to fast from the world and disconnect from the influences around you. The most profound teachers did just that, they fasted from the world for 40 days and 40 nights. I want to put emphasis on the importance of slowing down and stepping away from the material world so you can eliminate any attachment and grip it holds over you. This is the best way for you to truly evaluate where you really are in life and what path you should take to get where you really want to go.

If you need some basic logic to back up your choice in following the right path, there is the simple acid test that can be administered to the decision. Knowing a simple test will help you make the right decision in order to continue making progress in the right direction. Simply test the choices against, whether by following the information and guidelines does it cause anyone harm including myself? If it does not cause any harm, then there is no reason to not apply the principles in your life if it offers sound advice and a good meaningful way to live. If you think about it and it has a good sound foundation and no one can be harmed, then the potential gains far outweigh the losses as there are no losses. In that regard, the gains infinitely outweigh the alternative. Let's look at it another way, if you had a potential investment in stock where you have the potential for no losses, but yet have an infinite amount of potential gains I think that all investment planners would advise in investing in that stock plan. It is a win, win situation and it makes less logic to not invest, than to invest in this type of stock plan. There is a danger in over analyzing a decision, if you question it too long, negative thoughts will seep into your thinking and try to find a way to rationalize and justify why you should not do something that is good for you and everyone around you. Understand that there are always forces working against you trying to keep you from doing good. It is when we acknowledge and realize this truth that we make a decision to take that variable into account when we make decisions. Here is a passage in the bible that clearly illustrates the impact of the influences of the energies around us.

Romans 7:15 - ¹⁵ For I do not understand my own actions. For I do not do what I want, but I do the very thing I hate.

You will have similar experiences in life. You may be going through some of them now. You are not alone, for some reason sometimes we just do not do what we want to do and yet we do the thing we do not want to do. It could be something simple, like cutting back on junk food and candy or practicing your favorite sport to be better prepared for the next game. Maybe it is exercising so that we can be in better shape. The list goes on and for each person it may be completely different. It is when we realize that there is a negative force of energy that is influencing our very decisions that we can compel ourselves to do what we want and not what we hate. Anything is possible, even the eradication of bad habits or bad patterns of behavior. Once we realize that there is a silent attack happening in the form of negative energies influencing our feelings, we can be better on alert so we can recognize these feelings. Knowing this takes the power away from those bad energies as you will no longer be caught off guard on a sneak attack. You will be aware of what is happening around you and will realize what is most likely responsible for the feelings you are having. Being aware, you can better manage the actions you take based upon the knowledge that the feelings may not be coming from a positive force.

I want you to also know that sometimes we need to be willing to accept disruptions in what we expect to happen. Sometimes these events or situations are for our own benefit, even when we do not recognize it as such at the time. Do not jump to the conclusion that if something did not show up or materialize in your life the way you wanted it to it is because we attracted that situation due to an accumulation of bad energy. For example, we go to the grocery store to buy fruits and we wait in the cashier line. When we finally arrive to the cashier to pay, we are informed that the scale to weigh the fruit is broken and we have to go to another line. We may get angry or frustrated as we have to wait in line again. This type of situation may have been influenced in part by the disharmony in our ability to manifest and create the situation we wanted to have. We could have chosen any register, but we chose the one that has a broken scale. If we were living in harmony with life, we feel that we may have chosen a different line that was better. If we were truly living in unison with the will of God, we may realize immediately that the experience of getting delayed was what we needed at that exact moment for some reason. Rather than get angry or frustrated we would have recognized that we were experiencing this for a purpose and been grateful for it immediately. To continue the illustration, after we go in another line and pay, we go outside towards the car and realize there was a huge car accident minutes before as someone crashed from the road into the parking lot exactly where you would have been standing had you been able to check out with the first cashier. You realize then that God was working a miracle in your life causing that delay to keep you safe. Appreciate everything, for you may not know why you are experiencing something but there is always a reason.

What is important here is acceptance for the situation you are in. It is a gift that you are being made aware of the fact that you do have the ability to change and impact how you experience life. Not everyone will be given the ability to accept this truth into their belief system. Some lack faith, understanding or trust or maybe all of the above. Many when provided the details in this book will be blinded by their ego so they cannot see the truth. Be thankful if you do see the truth as that is a blessing.

As you eliminate the bad energies in your life and you follow a path to living by your true self, you will gain more freedoms and be more aware of the subtle energies that influence your decisions in life thereby being empowered to take control of your future back. You will be happier and alive. Depending on when you realize and accept this you may have to face additional growing pains to leave the cycle. Once you see the wonderful impact you have by owning your life and how if creates the reality you want to experience, you grow in confidence. You are given an opportunity to fulfill it the right way, it just becomes instinct to do things right. Deep down, we all want to be a good person anyway. In so doing, we can minimize or even totally eliminate the suffering experience unless we are being tested.

When we experience the freedom from walking through the pain, we have the added benefit of being in a position to help those around us and spread the message. We all have a life purpose, even if we have not realized it yet. You may be able to help someone realize their purpose or help someone understand how to truly live life and in the process you may learn something about you. Just having the opportunity to assist someone in realizing the truth in what we have discovered and the opportunity to assist someone to get back in touch with their primary purpose in life is a blessing, however do not force the message onto anyone. When talking to someone, if they are open to listening, then proceed. If they are completely against it, let it go and do not continue pursuing them. Dust your feet off so you do not absorb any of their negative energy. I want to take a side bar and point out that there are many references to washing your feet in the bible. Therefore, there must be some meaning behind it. Maybe it is to show servitude and humility as that is important in preventing the growth of the ego. May be it has multiple purposes and it is more than just symbolic. The ritualistic symbolism may have an effect on reality as we practice many rituals in life daily. In some theories the feet are thought to be used to ground us into the earth and the reality in which we live. If we have a bad ground or dirty ground, we do not get the energy needed to function properly. It may even impact the flow of energy around our body as anything would when you have a bad or dirty ground. Maybe by dusting off our feet from someone who does not want to listen to the truth, we prevent tracking their negative energy around or bringing it into contact with someone who does want to listen. If one purpose is for all of us is to raise our energy through the progression of working towards becoming positive thinking people or becoming a righteous person, then we want to rid ourselves of the negative influences. In order to do that, we may need to do this physically, ritualistically and spiritually.

Many times when we try to eliminate the bad influences, like eliminate a connection to someone who is no good for us they just seem to dig in harder and hold on as they feel you pulling away. They do it subconsciously, like somehow their ego knows to try and hold you down. They do not want to be alone and they feel themselves slipping further down. The old expression that misery loves company is so very true. Be strong and do what you need to do. By letting them stay attached to you, you may be preventing them from falling down to where they need to go in order to wear away their ego. It is not mean to let this happen. Maybe in order for them to grow they need to first fall in order for them to grow in their own way. By constantly being a buffer, you may be actually hurting them in the long run. As I mentioned the lessons will only get harder if people do not hear life calling. You may be enabling their ability to just barely stay afloat and not suffer enough to realize their true self. If you want to truly help them, show them the right way by acting the right way. By hanging out with them and encouraging their lousy behavior, you are not helping them. You do not need to feel obligated to laugh at vulgarities or participate in their bad behaviors or agree to their actions as they tell you about their drama in their life and how they acted.

In being strong and doing the right things, we accumulate even more spiritual gifts that in some way will assist us in dealing with these situations. As we grow in spiritual gifts, we are actually ascending to a higher spiritual existence and we attract higher energies into our very essence. As they see this happening in your life and they see their life falling apart, their true self may actually reach out without their ego and ask for help. They may ask for the right help finally, spiritual help and not help in the way of material things like money or a car. It is a blessing when you are able to help others in need and you can do so without being pulled down. Remember if you feel yourself being pulled down by someone you are trying to help, you will be of no use if you let them bring you down to their level. Sometimes you need to refer them to alternative places for help as you work on strengthening yourself.

I want for you to grow and live and I know as you develop a good heart, you will see how those around you are trapped. You may feel a calling and want to help, just pay attention that you are not falling down when you are trying to help. Remember that it is ok to get help from others if you need it, especially when trying to help someone else.

I am trying to provide as much guidance from what I have personally experienced to give you a strong foundation from where to grow and truly live life. My hope is that I have been able to make this as simple to understand and apply in your everyday life. In my quest for knowledge and wisdom, the common theme that seems to keep surfacing everywhere I look can be placed into these three basic principle core components. These three core principles are Trust, Forgiveness and Neighborly (TFN). I have heard alternative ways of describing similar methods: trust, clean house and help others. In context it is similar but not exact, so let us stay with Trust, Forgiveness and Neighborly (TFN) and you will see why as you read on.

I ask that as I continue trying to explain these truths and expand on the concepts in my own words that you please keep an open mind and listen to me thoroughly. I promise that when you understand what I understand, you will change inside and truly learn how to live. The challenge here is to get the message through to you so that you not only hear what I say but you also listen and decide to apply this in your everyday life. The farther off track you end up in life, "the dirtier your garment is" or the stronger your ego may have grown. This will just make it that much harder to get through to you to accept the truth. The exception to this is if you are currently suffering and your ego is eroding away right now. Depending how far away you are from the truth in life and how much you believe the lies will have a direct correlation to how strong your ego will try to defend its current belief system as the ego tries to remain in control of your life. Pray that this truth will find its way into your heart. You see, you can live a spiritual experience without your ego, but your ego cannot live without you and materialism.

Principle 1 - Trust

In my life endeavors, I have always been obsessed with what actually makes life work. I always felt that there had to be an underlining force that held everything together. I do not declare that I know everything and every aspect. Some of my experiences and the relationship stemming from the cause and effects are obvious once I put my ego aside and was willing to accept the truth. When we are able to step aside ourselves and take a look at ourselves from the eyes of an observer we can then determine why did certain events unfold and who or what did I trust at the time that situation manifested. What is truly remarkable is that the unseen and unknown force that holds everything in place provides so much order that it can at sometimes seem as though there was no order at all. The trust in the ultimate belief system allows for one to believe many different things all at once and not violate and rules or cause any paradoxes.

The key to knowledge is putting your trust in the right place as belief and faith differs based upon what you ultimately trust in. In truth, ones faith and belief do indeed have the ability to impact everything around a person so therefore, it is important to put your trust in the right place. Trusting the wrong ideology or source will ultimately cause turmoil in your life. The design from the ultimate architect of life is perfection beyond any imagination we could have dreamt of. I have looked at many different methods utilized to heal a person and minimize suffering, many of these programs touch on subjects related to the meaning of life and answers to questions on what life is. I have studied quantum physics and many different spiritual ideologies including the major religions of the world and new age spirituality. What I have learned the hard way is the fact that if some basic concepts are followed, we will just intuitively follow the right path.

The first principle of trust is so important, as without knowing who or what to trust we are lost. Imagine being in bed and not knowing if you can trust your senses that tell you that your bed is in the middle of a hard solid floor surface and not sitting on some weak thin sheet of paper above a lake full of hot lava. It would instill fear every time you took that first step out of bed in the morning, not knowing if you would land on a solid floor or if you would fall into the hot lava lake. What if you could not trust that when you go to school or work in the morning that your house or your bedroom would not disappear into another dimension? Going to school or work would be a little scary not knowing what will be there for you at the end of the day. You see, first is trust. We must have trust in order to just survive without being paralyzed by fear. We must have trust in order to have faith and believe in the right methodology. To put it simply, lack of trust keeps a person in fear and ignorant of the truth. If you trust in the right source then the faith and belief that follows will lead you in the right direction, always. Faith and belief continually grows from trusting in the right source, it just happens that way. It is something you just know is right in your heart.

What hangs most people up is whether we want to accept it, as there are implications to acknowledging the truth. We inevitably must change our behaviors to bring our actions in alignment with our true selves. Some people are so in debt to sin that they find it hard to do and do not know where to get help to make that change. The feeling(s) that tells us what is right from wrong, actually comes from connections in our heart to the subconscious. It can be thought of as a higher self directing us in life, but we have to slow down and listen. When we do, we then just intuitively know what is true. Knowing truth will help us live in light and not darkness.

Another way to think about the idea of just knowing what is right from wrong is that it is coming from our collective consciousness. Collectively, we are very intelligent which is why we need to treat each other with respect and learn to work together. The collective conscious is called many different things in many societies and cultures. The fundamental nature of the collective consciousness is a field energy that we can tap into to gain access to all knowledge and information of everything that has happened, is happening or can happen. If you want to understand the process by where the collective conscious works, there is information on this subject everywhere. One fascinating piece of information related to understanding the collective conscious is the 100th monkey experiment. It shows a leap of consciousness that can only be explained by supernatural means as it defied logical explanations when the behaviors were first observed. I want to also add that we do have multiple layers of consciousness. The multiple layers can start with our immediate family, to friends and co-workers to groups and associations up through race, religions and countries and so on.

In some remote viewing programs that the US government and military was involved with it is called the matrix, in some new age spiritual programs that draw on ancient texts, it is called the Akashic records. No matter what you call it, it is defining the same knowledge base of consciousness that we have access to. The key that unlocks its secret is the ability to slow down in life. To understand, you need to match the frequencies of love through the appreciation of life for what it is. It is like tuning in the radio station in your mind to the station of unconditional love. You have to filter out all other influences and through deep meditative states you will tune into something that is not describable in words but when you do, you know it. In this process, somehow knowledge is downloaded and you have access to this knowledge from that point forward. This key will keep those not ready away from ever understanding the truth for you must know love and have it in your heart first.

The most common method for accessing this knowledge is through intention in your prayer and meditation. You must be resilient when you meditate. Even if you only get a brief second of that complete inner peace, keep at it and with practice you will be able to hold the tuner in your mind longer and longer to this frequency and thereby absorb more. In order to properly know who to pray to and listen to during meditation, you have to know who to trust and believe in. You may at times have full recollection of events and conversations. As time progresses they will become stronger and you will remember them consciously. The lie many believe, is that it is hard to connect and meditate. The truth is with love and the right intention anyone can do it. There is even a special form of meditation they call "Stillness", which is a combined form of prayer and meditation in a very relaxed setting. I recommend researching this form as a way to start learning about meditation and communion with God through prayer.

When you pray and trust in the right source you can just feel it is true, it emanates a feeling of love that overpowers you. I am not talking about walking on a pink cloud. The pink cloud feeling is a false happiness that the ego trying to trick you with. It is trying to distract you and make you feel that you are connected, so you can keep going on about your daily life as there is no need to mediate anymore. Be resilient and look into your heart for answers, keep praying and meditating. If you have a revelation, recall a message or remember a conversation in some way, write it down so you will always remember it.

When trying to validate what or who you should trust, use the acid test. Start by looking at the teachings. You can ask yourself if the teachings learned from trusting that source lead you into darkness or light. The answer is obvious, but again if the ego is too strong it will keep you from understanding this fact. This is why it is important to know that there is a force working against you from listening to the truth. It tries to prevent truth from penetrating into your heart where you can connect and validate itself on its own merits. The ego knows that the heart is the best place to plant something that will grow strong, so it fights hard to keep the truth away. You have to be willing to peel away the layers of the ego which can be exasperated when surrounded by materialism. When you finally truly listen without responding or reacting and absorb the truth into your heart, it changes you from within. You have to listen to the entire message in its entirety, not just the parts your current belief system likes. We have to be open minded. We may have to adopt new philosophies to match the new truths we have just learned. We have to recognize that trust, faith and belief are intertwined and with the right source, anything is possible. I want to reference words of wisdom on the importance of faith in the bible, remember in order to put your faith into something you have to trust it. I recommend reading the entire passage on faith in Hebrews 11, but here is an excerpt.

Hebrews 11:1-3 [11] *Now faith is the assurance of things hoped for, the conviction of things not seen.* [2] *For by it the people of old received their commendation.* [3] *By faith we understand that the universe was created by the word of God, so that what is seen was not made out of things that are visible.*

Trusting of the correct ideology allows for us to put our faith in the right hands and believe in the teachings provided and methodology used. This is critical for in choosing the wrong ideology, even when the alternative methodology sounds like the same thing, the teachings from it can be detrimental in the long run. Following the wrong discipline will eventually lead you far away from where we want to be. Look at this passage from the bible warning us to be prudent in what you put your trust in.

2 Timothy 4:3-5 [3] *For there will be a time when they will not put up with sound teaching, but in accordance with their own desires, they will accumulate for themselves teachers, because they have an insatiable curiosity,* [4] *and they will turn away from the hearing of the truth, but will turn to myths.* [5] *But you, be self-controlled in all things, bear hardship patiently, do the work of an evangelist, fulfill your ministry.*

Most methodologies or spiritual programs do seem at the surface to be saying the same thing, but they are not. Without getting too much into what I have experienced, let me explain at a high level my point. As I studied other program teachings and ideologies I learned that if the alternate ideologies are only mostly correct, for instance let's say 80% correct, that leaves 20% incorrect information. Logically then, if we apply the alternative ideologies learned in these other programs with the 80% accuracy level, that left 20% of the information and teachings wrong. I want to clearly state, that even if at first the program looks promising by creating wonderful and profound changes in your life they may plateau and eventually lead you further away from the truth as they most likely were designed that way. The reality is that if 20% of the time the ideology is wrong it will cause harm in the long run as you do not know when to trust the teachings and when not to trust them. Think about this; why would you want to put your full faith and trust into something that only works 80% of the time? You would be stuck living in a world of uncertainly and fear, knowing that just around the corner there is a chance that what you put your trust in may fail.

Providing the wrong ideology and teaching is similar to providing disinformation to your enemy for the purpose of sabotaging them. This type of tactic has been utilized in war in order to gain your enemy's trust to believe and have faith in the source and information that is provided to them on purpose. Typically, in a war when implementing this tactic, someone will provide quality information most of the time but will sprinkle it with bad information. That disinformation is what can kill the enemy or lead them to capture. This is like relying on the wrong source of information and being infested with negative energy, whereby you are led into total darkness and sin to the point of eventually running out of credit and the only way to pay off your debt is with your very soul. If anyone trusts the 80/20 percent accuracy of the information as being completely reliable and 100% accurate, it is easy to lead that person into their own demise. What is worse, is that the ego will be perfectly happy with going down with the ship, since another weakness of the ego is the desire to be right at all cost. In its inability to let you admit you are wrong and made a mistake, the ego can have such a grip on you that it makes the believable unbelievable and the unbelievable believable. This was a huge fallacy of mine, pride and my inability to keep my ego in check prevented me for so long in seeing where I was wrong as I custom built my ideologies and teaching rather than using what was true. To admit when you have trusted the wrong belief system is a blessing, it gives you time to make an adjustment in life without suffering. I do not want to deviate too far into the concept of blessing and reprieve at this time, however life does throw us a chance to correct our path and direction in life, most of us do not realize it.

I want you to focus on what is true and what is 100% accurate. That is the teaching and messages left by the son of God, Jesus Christ. Jesus testifies to the truth and provides for the witnesses to validate the testimony. What I have discovered if you could not tell already is that the information in the bible is true. Some of it is clear to understand at first reading, some writing is veiled in a way that prevents many from understanding its content at first glance. The fact is that when you are ready, it will all read as plain as day. You have to keep searching and reading because by doing so, the bible comes alive. You realize the terminology is static and used over and over in various writings by different authors. In very few circumstances are the terms used dynamic and change substantially. Even when it does change, the literature itself defines what is meant by what was written. I want to give you a jump start on what to trust so you can eliminate the time wasted in searching or trying the wrong spiritual programs. I would not lead you in the wrong direction and therefore what I say is true and from my heart.

I discovered that we must Trust in Jesus Christ, it is everywhere and yet many do not see it. I know the bible is lengthy and it does take time to read through it all. Listening to it or watching accurate videos where the message was not modified in any way is a great way to start absorbing the protection the bible offers us by arming ourselves with the truth. Understand that parts of the bible are designed to hide information from those not deemed worthy to understand it. It has many hidden and veiled messages all over that are remarkable and help validate the truth of the word in it. The vast wealth of knowledge in the bible is amazing and yet we let our ego tell us what part we want to accept and what part we want to try and rationalize or justify in a way to suit our lifestyle. Each time I read it, I learn more or understand something with greater wisdom. I recommend that you to study it, but for now I want to point out the most important ideology I learned from the bible, which is to trust in Jesus Christ. If you read the bible more, it will explain and show you reasons why this is true. What is critical to understand here is the importance of using the right roadmap in life. When you trust and use the right map, getting to the place you want to go is far easier without getting lost on the way. When you couple this first principle with the remaining other two principles, you will have a firm foundation that will keep you heading in the right direction no matter what life may test you with. Sometimes the test comes in the form of temptation. Know that you always have a choice and a way to escape its grasp. Read again the below passage on temptation.

1 Corinthians 10:12-13 [13] *No temptation has overtaken you that is not common to man. God is faithful, and he will not let you be tempted beyond your ability, but with the temptation he will also provide the way of escape, that you may be able to endure it.*

When you realize all the tools you have available by seeking God's wisdom and knowledge, it is impossible to fail with God helping you though it all. This is why I find the truth to these basic principles to be so imperative to life that I want to create a strong foundation for you to grow from. Take the time to expand your knowledge and read on your own more than just the few passages I copied into this book.

Principle 2 - Forgiveness

Forgiveness is next. We must rid ourselves of all the guilt in the way of debt incurred by sinning against each other. Failure to do this will destroy us as it causes energy flow disruptions in spiritual form that eventually manifests in the physical world in different ways. In order to do this, we need to forgive everyone first and ask to be forgiven for everything we did. When we sin the fact is that we are sinning against someone in some way. There is no sin that does not hurt someone, believing that you can sin and not hurt someone is a lie the ego tells us. It is the ego that justifies and says certain sins are ok in order to get what it wants. We can try to justify it and say things like, it doesn't really hurt anyone. The fact is that someone always gets hurt when we sin, most notably ourselves. That is important as you always know right from wrong and you are keeping track of everything that you do subconsciously.

When we accumulate this sin debt or obligation, it must be paid back. Everything has to balance. If we have an open trespass against someone we are obligated to make good on it or we carry this debt until we do make good on it. This debt impacts our ability to live. In addition, when someone trespasses against you they incur a debt or obligation to you that must be paid back. No one gets away with anything; this is the crux of how life unfolds. There are checks and balances in life, we just choose to ignore and disbelief the truth as the lies are easier to swallow and accept, plus it allows for our ego to get what it wants. It is easier to cast blame on someone else for the problems we experience in life and not admit that through disharmonious energy fluctuations we created the very life we are living. We bare the sins and transgressions we commit against others and because of this, we have difficulty achieving happiness in life. Our energy flow is hampered by this debt in some way. We cannot lie to ourselves as we are the record keepers of our own actions and we know right from wrong. If we didn't know right from wrong, we could not sin. Remember in the bible we are taught in genesis about the tree knowledge and how by knowing right from wrong we will die and we do spiritually when we fail to do right.

Genesis 3:3 - ³ but of the fruit of the tree which is in the midst of the garden, God hath said, Ye shall not eat of it, neither shall ye touch it, lest ye die.

This should give you a different perspective on life and why you should always do the right thing. Don't let the ego rationalize or justify your actions. If you look deep within yourself, you always know what is right from wrong and you have to understand that there are always consequences, even if they are not immediate. Again, if you need to use the acid test mentioned earlier by looking at what would Jesus do in that situation please do. Do not let yourself be fooled by bad energies, use the bible as your shield when facing adversity. This is what they mean many times when they say sharpen the sword of your tongue with the word of God. I found this reference in the bible many times. When you understand and accept that you cannot run away from the simple fact that you owe a debt for the trespasses against each other, you will try with all the solemnity available to stop sinning and to find a way to be relieved of your sins you have committed already. These sins or debts in the way of guilt weigh on us and accumulate over time. The ill effects may not be easily visible at first, but over time you will realize how it is impacting your life. Feel blessed if you feel guilt over the slightest infraction as that is a good sign that you have not been desensitized to our real feelings. Be thankful then that you still have an ability to connect to God and each other spiritually through love and kindness.

I consider this sensitivity to our surroundings a form of meekness. Much of my life I was highly sensitive to people around me. I wore my heart on my sleeve and I was told to put it away. Even in movies at certain scenes of love or sadness, I would have tears in my eyes and have to hide. Around certain situations I can feel the pain or the happiness of those around me. I could also feel the anger or frustrations of people. I could feel their true intentions. This is a good thing as it opens you up to compassion and understanding when talking with people and it keeps you safe from certain people. Embrace this gift and do not hide it. Too much negative energy and the disruptions in energy flows causes static on the station of life when we are tuning in. Because of this, many do not feel compassion or they bury those feelings for fear of ridicule. That makes it hard to pick up the signals from life which can be in the form of guilt that will help guide us in life. The negative energy is the cause of much suffering. As you read in the bible more and more, the evidence is clear. You have to be released of this debt to be healed as the more negative energy you accumulate impacts your physical world by manifesting not just problems in life for you to face, but real physical or mental illnesses, even diseases that can incapacitate you. There is evidence of this all over the bible, we just have to read what was written. If you look carefully in the bible, whenever someone is miraculously healed in the bible we also can see the term of forgiveness of sins or casting out the evil spirits or demons used too. One way I think about negative energy is that it can be considered a demon, as it causes blockages in our energy flow. It is like a leach, sucking away our life force and causing all kinds of short circuits in our body. Allowing too much bad energy into our self is like letting demons into our soul that eat away at it as they consume it, for that is the way they survive. Look at these passages from the bible.

Acts 19:11-13 [11] And God was doing extraordinary miracles by the hands of Paul, [12] so that even handkerchiefs or aprons that had touched his skin were carried away to the sick, and their diseases left them and the evil spirits came out of them.

Mark 1:32-33 [32] That evening after sunset, many sick and demon-possessed people were brought to Jesus. [33] The whole town gathered at the door to watch. [34] So Jesus healed many people who were sick with various diseases, and he cast out many demons. But because the demons knew who he was, he did not allow them to speak.

Mark2:9-11 [9] Which is easier, to say to the paralytic, 'Your sins are forgiven,' or to say, 'Rise, take up your bed and walk'? [10] But that you may know that the Son of Man has authority on earth to forgive sins"— he said to the paralytic— [11] "I say to you, rise, pick up your bed, and go home."

Mathew 4:23-24 [23] And he went throughout all Galilee, teaching in their synagogues and proclaiming the gospel of the kingdom and healing every disease and every affliction among the people. [24] So his fame spread throughout all Syria, and they brought him all the sick, those afflicted with various diseases and pains, those oppressed by demons, epileptics, and paralytics, and he healed them.

If you continue to read as I hope you do, you will see for yourself how evil and bad energies go hand in hand with disease and illness. It makes perfect sense when we relate to energy flows in and around our spiritual form and how the negative energies ultimately manifest problems for us in our physical form. This in itself should be enough motivation to keep you and people around us from sinning against each other. The issue is people's inability to accept the truth as the ego is defending their current beliefs. Ultimately, if they do not know or they do not believe the right truth then they would see no need to change their ways. Don't be like them, don't remain ignorant. Take advantage of the wealth of knowledge and wisdom available for free, all we have to do is seek it out from the right source. If you listened to what I mentioned in the first principle, you already know to put your trust in Jesus.

I want you to know that not all calamities people experience in life are a direct result of sins, the following passage clarifies that and eliminates any confusion but it also, as in other places in the bible, it clearly shows that a person can accumulate so much debt they never were relieved from, that it may manifest in future generations, possibly in their own children. I am doing everything possible to remove all debt so as to never pass anything on to anyone. I would much rather find a way to clear the path for everyone if possible.

John 9:1-3 *¹ As he passed by, he saw a man blind from birth. ² And his disciples asked him, "Rabbi, who sinned, this man or his parents, that he was born blind?" ³ Jesus answered, "It was not that this man sinned, or his parents, but that the works of God might be displayed in him.*

I want to go at a high level and think about our very soul and the life experiences we create. These experiences in life truly help shape and define us. It is our memories and our ability to draw on those past experiences in making decisions in present everyday activities possible. These experiences are information and we store them in our conscious mind. We draw upon these experiences in order to understand and interpret the world we know. If we are drowning in sin and guilt, and surrounded by negative energy we have to clear it all away and be debt free by applying the second principle and forgiving each other. If we all ask for forgiveness and we all forgive each other, no one would have any debt. We would all be free as nothing would be holding us back from reaching a higher energy level. So, if we apply the first principle which is to trust in Jesus and apply the second principle which is forgiveness we can all be freed of our debt. The only other attachments to the physical world would then be materialism and ego, and in order to understand much of what I have written here, you should already be freeing yourself of ego and materialism if you have not already.

I want to point out that Jesus even provided us a way out even when we accumulate so much debt in the way of guilt from sin that it would seem like we could never pay it off. He paid the ransom to free us from this debt obligation with his life. You see, unpaid debt on a secured loan means you lose your security if you are unable to pay it back. The debt we incur with the sins we accumulate is secured with our soul, if we do not pay it back we lose it. So if we are unable to make things right with each other directly we can still ask for forgiveness through faith and trust in Jesus Christ. We just need to know how and where to go. You are fortunate if you have been baptized and have or plan on receiving the sacraments of reconciliation, first communion and confirmation or others if you so choose. It is important to understand how these sacraments transform you and why they are there. If you are helping someone, lead them to a place where they can learn about the importance of them. Not everyone has gone through the sacraments or fully understand how powerful they are, what they are and what they can do for you. They are available for those that want them. Anyone can go to their local church and ask about them, lead them there when asked. That is all that Jesus Christ conditions this saving grace on, that we trust in him and ask for forgiveness. Just think how wonderful it is that that all we have to do is understand the process well enough to receive the sacraments so that we can receive his saving grace. You may not truly realize that through his crucifixion and his sacrifice of his own flesh and blood, he paid the debt obligation on all the sins out of his love for us. His dying on the cross was the payment of all debt accumulated through sins. As a perfect man, his energy was so pure and clean that it was worth so much that it covered the debt for all our sins.

Forgiveness requires death in some way, death of the obligation to repay the debt from sin. By sacrificing himself, he makes a new covenant with us. He loved us that much that he paid the ultimate price. By doing so, he uses mercy to relieve us of our debts. This information can be found in a few places in the bible, I copied in a couple of longer passages. I want for you to do your own reading to gain a better understanding if you so choose.

Mathew 26:26-28 ²⁶ Now as they were eating, Jesus took bread, and after blessing it broke it and gave it to the disciples, and said, "Take, eat; this is my body." ²⁷ And he took a cup, and when he had given thanks he gave it to them, saying, "Drink of it, all of you, ²⁸ for this is my blood of the covenant, which is poured out for many for the forgiveness of sins.

Hebrews 9:11-21 ¹¹ But Christ has arrived as a high priest of the good things to come. Through the greater and more perfect tent not made by hands, that is, not of this creation, ¹² and not by the blood of goats and calves, but by his own blood, he entered once for all into the most holy place, obtaining eternal redemption. ¹³ For if the blood of goats and bulls and the ashes of a young cow sprinkled on those who are defiled sanctify them for the ritual purity of the flesh, ¹⁴ how much more will the blood of Christ, who through the eternal Spirit offered himself without blemish to God, cleanse our consciences from dead works to serve the living God? *[15] And because of this, he is the mediator of a new covenant, in order that, because a death has taken place for the redemption of transgressions committed during the first covenant, those who are the called may receive the promise of the eternal inheritance. [16] For where there is a will, it is a necessity for the death of the one who made the will to be established. [17] For a will is in force concerning those who are dead, since it is never in force when the one who made the will is alive. [18] Therefore not even the first covenant was ratified without blood. [19] For when every commandment had been spoken by Moses to all the people according to the law, he took the blood of calves with water and scarlet wool and hyssop and sprinkled both the scroll itself and all the people, [20] saying, "This is the blood of the covenant that God has commanded for you." [21] And likewise he sprinkled both the tabernacle and all the utensils of service with the blood. [22] Indeed, nearly everything is purified with blood according to the law, and apart from the shedding of blood there is no forgiveness.*

I feel that this is important, for Jesus gives us all an opportunity to clean up our past and no longer sin. The only stipulation to receiving forgiveness is that we must forgive all others of their debt to us, regardless of their trespass to us. This stipulation is crucial. I know friends that have seen some improvement in their life, but they still feel like they carry a large burden after they asked for forgiveness. The truth is they did not forgive everyone else so they have not been forgiven of all their sins. They are still holding onto a resentment which is holding them back. Know that resentments will hurt you, holding onto that resentment prevents you from being released of all your debt. You see the old way to achieve righteousness was through the law, and the new way is through mercy. If you want mercy to be granted to you, then you must be willing to give mercy to others freely. Here are a couple passages, but again I ask that you take it upon yourself to read more into this.

Romans 7:7-12 [7] What then shall we say? Is the law sin? May it never be! But I would not have known sin except through the law, for I would not have known covetousness if the law had not said, "Do not covet." [8] But sin, seizing an opportunity through the commandment, produced in me all kinds of covetousness. For apart from the law, sin is dead. [9] And I was alive once, apart from the law, but when the commandment came, sin sprang to life [10] and I died, and this commandment which was to lead to life was found with respect to me to lead to death. [11] For sin, seizing the opportunity through the commandment, deceived me and through it killed me. [12] So then, the law is holy, and the commandment is holy and righteous and good.

Mathew 9:10-13 [10] And as Jesus reclined at table in the house, behold, many tax collectors and sinners came and were reclining with Jesus and his disciples. [11] And when the Pharisees saw this, they said to his disciples, "Why does your teacher eat with tax collectors and sinners?" [12] But when he heard it, he said, "Those who are well have no need of a physician, but those who are sick. [13] Go and learn what this means, 'I desire mercy, and not sacrifice.' For I came not to call the righteous, but sinners."

The shedding of blood and all the laws from Moses in the old testament was to help us achieve righteousness, but as we can see in our own inability to adhere to the law we created more sin. There are certain laws or covenants that exist that must be adhered to, and while I do not want to go too far into the subject of all the sacrifices in the old testament to eliminate the negative energies we accumulated through sin, it is clearly apparent what was being done and why. The Jews weren't the only people offering sacrifices in the world in the past. Mayans and other cultures had been doing this for years, and in those cultures it was an honor to be chosen as the sacrifice for the spiritual rewards were believed to be great. You can study this on your own, but I did want to touch on why the Old Testament had so much bloodshed, wars, sacrifice and laws. When and if you read it, it will become apparent that we were on a collision course with total destruction as we kept breaking the laws and sinning.

We were in a battle to rid the influences of the negative energies and a battle to remain righteous and not accumulate new debt in the way of sin. With so many laws that existed, it was easy to break them and continue slipping further into self destruction. What happened next is important, Jesus came along and created a new covenant and became our mediator, and the interpreter of the laws, for what better person to mediate than the son of God. For Jesus will be seated at the right hand of the father to judge the living and the dead. I urge you to read more than just the passages I have copied below. Seek the proper knowledge and wisdom as it will explain much about the old and the New Testament, but here is what I copied from the bible.

1 Timothy 2:1-6 ¹ First of all, then, I urge that supplications, prayers, intercessions, and thanksgivings be made for all people, ² for kings and all who are in high positions, that we may lead a peaceful and quiet life, godly and dignified in every way. ³ This is good, and it is pleasing in the sight of God our Savior, ⁴ who desires all people to be saved and to come to the knowledge of the truth. ⁵ For there is one God, and there is one mediator between God and men, the man Christ Jesus, ⁶ who gave himself as a ransom for all, which is the testimony given at the proper time.

It seems that in order to pay for the debt of sin, something valuable had to be exchanged in order to cover the ransom for all of us. If physical matter, and I mean the persons physical body with all its mass and energy associated with it can be broken down into individual atoms, and we know that atoms when split release a large amount of energy, could it be the value from such a righteous person was a large amount of energy in a way that released us from being a slave to sin? This I do not know, I only speculate when I hear things like as above, so below and relate it to many things. I will even think in terms of the drive for energy here and how who has control of it here on the planet seems to own and control so much on Earth. I want to add too, something intriguing related to an old thought experiment which was created 150 years ago known as Maxwell's demon. I saw an article that his experiment was proved possible in the last few years. What this demon does is convert information into energy. I do not want to go into the intricacies of it as I have not fully dissected it, but it is a strange anomaly. As you will find I no longer believe in chance. Everything does happen for a reason, it is when we stop being afraid to face the reasons that we can gain wisdom and knowledge through learning and in so doing, acceptance that the situation is in our life for a reason.

I want to touch on other ways we can further stay clear of negative energies. We can pray for help and compassion and understanding. Praying and being thankful for what you have is important as it eliminates desires for things of the flesh. Praying before a meal and giving thanks for the meal clears the negative energies that the food has been contact with. Eliminating certain foods is really not necessary, as everything that God created is good. Here is a little passage from the bible, but go ahead and read on.

1 Timothy 4:4-5 [4] For everything created by God is good, and nothing is to be rejected if it is received with thanksgiving, [5] for it is made holy by the word of God and prayer.

Stay away from wicked people who only think about themselves. Those people who are so self absorbed with the materialistic world have no sense of what is true. Stay away, but offer prayer for them when you encounter them. Stay clear of greedy people who worship money, do not let their false beliefs and lies corrupt your thoughts. There are so many ways to keep your-self clean and on the right path. Here is a passage in the bible, but please read more on your own.

Luke 16:13 [13] *No servant can serve two masters, for either he will hate the one and love the other, or he will be devoted to the one and despise the other. You cannot serve God and money."*

Mathew 19:24 [24] *Again I tell you, it is easier for a camel to go through the eye of a needle than for a rich person to enter the kingdom of God."*

I have showed you just a few areas to avoid, one being the love of money as it has ruined many souls. It is for the weak minded, as they see value in material things and seek immediate satisfaction to satisfy their cravings for physical desires. They think they can satisfy their cravings with money, but it can never be satisfied. You need to realize that and not fall for the lure and lies associated with money. Those that care about money so much cannot see spiritual things. Money will not buy you an entrance pass into heaven. It is actually a blessing to be poor, for you would not have all the worries of the materialistic world clogging your ability to slow down in life and realize what is truly important. Fear of ridicule or loss of identity and materialism will keep negative people away from realizing the truth. I am not saying it is impossible to enter into heaven if you have money, for with God all things are possible. Just know that with money comes additional responsibility to not let it lead your life and control what you do and how you behave as you will be held accountable for everything you do in life.

Principle 3 - Neighborly

The golden rule is the last of the three principles, but not least important. After you went through the process of being released of all the debt, the last thing you would want to do is incur more debt. In order to do that, you need to not trespass against anyone and sin again. The best method for this I have found, is implementing the golden rule. Treat your neighbors as you want to be treated, treat your neighbor as yourself. The concept is easy to implement and it is easy to understand the philosophy behind it. If you treat others as yourself, you intuitively would do no wrong to anyone. By not sinning against anyone, you no longer incur any new debt from sinning against each other. It is truly simple to think about; why would you harm yourself or why would you incur debt to yourself? The answer is obvious, you wouldn't. Just like you cannot lie to yourself, you cannot secure and incur a debt to yourself by yourself. There is no reason to. This solution is obvious once we realize it. If we want to stop the vicious cycle that tears away at our soul, you would follow the golden rule and treat your neighbor as yourself. Remember that as we accumulate debt in the way of sins and transgressions, the guilt secured is against our soul. It always needs to balance and be paid back either through forgiveness of the debt or through death of the debt. Failure to pay it back causes us to lose our soul. Know this to be true, once you have gone through the process of forgiving all others of their debt and you go to confession and ask to be forgiven of your debts, as long as you stop the cycle of accumulating new debt you can truly live and no longer be a slave to sin. Treating your neighbor as yourself from this point on is one of the best ways of staying debt free and owning your soul free and clear. Here it is in the bible, please take the time to read and understand these truths.

Mathew 7:12 [12] *"So whatever you wish that others would do to you, do also to them, for this is the Law and the Prophets.*

The golden rule is good when followed, but many do not adhere completely to its teaching. They pick and choose when they will act neighborly and to whom they will treat as themselves. They choose to be neighborly only to people that they feel are nice or that treat them nicely. Realize that this philosophy of partial adherence of this principal is doomed from the start. This is the path most take as it is the easiest to justify conditional behavior with, but that is not what Jesus is telling us. He is telling us at this point to always treat your neighbor the way you want to be treated, regardless of the circumstance. Following that protocol is more challenging, as you have to walk a tight rope as there is little room for error. In the very next passage we get confirmation of this.

Mathew 7:13 [13] *"Enter by the narrow gate. For the gate is wide and the way is easy that leads to destruction, and those who enter by it are many.* [14] *For the gate is narrow and the way is hard that leads to life, and those who find it are few.*

As I stated previously, what makes this concept so challenging to put into motion is when it seems that someone is doing us wrong. We want revenge or to snap and react to that person. What I can say here, is no matter what, do what we are told by Jesus and turn the other cheek. Do not retaliate under any circumstance, have faith that God will handle them. In other words, do not get back or even with someone for wrong doings to you. It is important to stay away from trying to get even, as this will surely keep you in constant resentment as you compare who did who more wrong. The following passage explains this in detail and makes perfect sense.

Romans 12: 17-21 - [17] Repay no one evil for evil, but give thought to do what is honorable in the sight of all. [18] If possible, so far as it depends on you, live peaceably with all. [19] Beloved, never avenge yourselves, but leave it to the wrath of God, for it is written, "Vengeance is mine, I will repay, says the Lord." [20] To the contrary, "if your enemy is hungry, feed him; if he is thirsty, give him something to drink; for by so doing you will heap burning coals on his head." [21] Do not be overcome by evil, but overcome evil with good.

Understand too that I am not telling you to put yourself out there to get yourself abused. I just want you to know the right option as there is no need to bring yourself down to someone else's level and fight back by adding more injustices. Try to eliminate the bad influence, walk away or disconnect from that source of negative influence. Don't let it pollute you, you have that option. It is not weak to do this. It is more powerful than you can imagine and it becomes readily apparent after just a few times of practicing this approach when dealing with negative people, places or things. Remember, even if you have been wronged, forgive and pray for them and leave that negative influence to its own demise, God will see it so. That's the way it works in life if you let it. Remember, no one gets away with anything.

I learned the hard way with many of these lessons. One fact that stands out for me that will help you stay clear of the potholes in the road while traveling through life, is the importance of treating everyone with respect. It does not matter who they are or what they do for a living, treat them with respect. I have a high regard now for individuals that take on those hard jobs. I am even more amazed that many do the tough jobs and enjoy their work. They take on the jobs that other people don't want to do and appreciate the work. As you grow in life you will meet and work with all kinds of people. Sometimes you meet people that somehow you just know are filled with a good spirit, strangers even. I look back at life and realize that many times I interacted with the right person at the right time and they were trying to send me a message. I may not have always known it at the time. Maybe the truth I was told at the time, I did not like or want to hear, but it was exactly what I needed at the time I needed. It is the other force, a guiding force, a good force that is also at work trying to help us and keep us on the right path. Therefore, remember to always treat everyone with honor and respect. Be willing to serve others for you never know as the person you serve very well maybe the person trying to save your very soul.

Hebrews 13:1-2 ¹ *Let brotherly love continue.* ² *Do not neglect to show hospitality to strangers, for thereby some have entertained angels unawares.*

Stay away from judging people under any circumstance, for in so doing you open yourself to be judged in the same way. I know that I have made many mistakes in my life and looking back at it now, it is seemingly apparent that some force was constantly trying to throw stumbling block in my way. This was the bad force. That bad, negative force was influencing me to be lover of self, ego and money so that I would not love God. I constantly fell for the traps and was easily tempted. This is what I want for you to learn, that there is a negative force that is trying to cause us to fail or be distracted by lies. When you do understand this and you are going down the right road, before you decide to judge or tell someone else what they are doing wrong, take another look at yourself. See where you can improve first. Now I do not say that if someone asks you for help you do not point them in the right direction. I am just talking about the lure of wanting to provide unsolicited help to someone by throwing stones at them and telling them where they fall short without first careful examination of your own faults. It is best to let people come to you. I have found that even when I see something that can be helpful to someone else, I may not know the full story of their circumstance. By assuming anything and then approaching that person unsolicited, their ego may very well put up a brick wall preventing them from hearing anything anyway. Here are a couple passages from the bible.

Mathew 7:1-5 [1] *"Judge not, that you be not judged.* [2] *For with the judgment you pronounce you will be judged, and with the measure you use it will be measured to you.* [3] *Why do you see the speck that is in your brother's eye, but do not notice the log that is in your own eye?* [4] *Or how can you say to your brother, 'Let me take the speck out of your eye,' when there is the log in your own eye?* [5] *You hypocrite, first take the log out of your own eye, and then you will see clearly to take the speck out of your brother's eye.*

Remember that in helping someone who still has a brick wall up, they have to tear it down. If it does not come down through suffering, it must be taken down delicately. Just try to imagine that you have a house that everyone around you knows it is damaged badly and that it needs to be condemned, torn down and rebuilt. If someone came over and started a fire to burn my house down, even if in the long run it is what is needed, I would stay and fight to keep my structure up. I would spray water on the fire and put it out. Then I probably would never let my friend come over again, as from my perspective he wants to destroy my house. Rather what is needed is a careful plan to empower me to want to take my house apart, maybe brick by brick so that I can rebuild it properly. We can help others, but we have to be delicate in helping them take down their ego if they are not suffering. I would want someone to try that approach for me if it was obvious that my "house" or ego needed to be torn down and rebuilt.

We are constantly told that we need to treat each other with kindness, even strangers. This similar theme is in many places in the bible. Jesus is telling us a similar theme and many different ways. He is telling us that whatsoever you do to the least of my brothers, that you do onto me. That should make you wonder what all that means and why it is so important to treat your neighbor as yourself. Please take the time to understand this and read more on this as it is what will truly help you stay on course. The references to this truth is everywhere, seek and ye shall find. I have a couple passages from the bible to look at, but continue on your own. You may learn something you can teach me.

Mathew 25:35-40 [35] *For I was hungry and you gave me food, I was thirsty and you gave me drink, I was a stranger and you welcomed me,* [36] *I was naked and you clothed me, I was sick and you visited me, I was in prison and you came to me.'* [37] *Then the righteous will answer him, saying, 'Lord, when did we see you hungry and feed you, or thirsty and give you drink?* [38] *And when did we see you a stranger and welcome you, or naked and clothe you?* [39] *And when did we see you sick or in prison and visit you?'* [40] *And the King will answer them, 'Truly, I say to you, as you did it to one of the least of these my brothers, you did it to me.'*

Acts 9:1-9 But Saul, still breathing threats and murder against the disciples of the Lord, went to the high priest [2] *and asked him for letters to the synagogues at Damascus, so that if he found any belonging to the Way, men or women, he might bring them bound to Jerusalem.* [3] *Now as he went on his way, he approached Damascus, and suddenly a light from heaven shone around him. ⁴ And falling to the ground he heard a voice saying to him, "Saul, Saul, why are you persecuting me?" ⁵ And he said, "Who are you, Lord?" And he said, "I am Jesus, whom you are persecuting. ⁶ But rise and enter the city, and you will be told what you are to do." ⁷ The men who were traveling with him stood speechless, hearing the voice but seeing no one. ⁸ Saul rose from the ground, and although his eyes were opened, he saw nothing. So they led him by the hand and brought him into Damascus.*

It is amazing how Christ can come alive in us through the Holy Spirit if we ask for and seek him out. When we seek out truth, something just happens that guides us to where we need to go to find it. When we learn to trust our instinct and follow our heart honestly in an effort to do good, good will find us. I do not want to say that there is still no testing that may come my way, but I will be better prepared. Understanding how Jesus Christ is alive in spirit and how with the Holy Spirit he can enter under our roof, then the proposition of treating our neighbors as ourselves becomes easier and easier to do. We can look not to condemn those that trespass against us, but to feel compassion and pray for them to wake up so they too can be healed and live free and not a slave to sin.

1 Peter 3:18-19 ¹⁸ For Christ also suffered once for sins, the righteous for the unrighteous, that he might bring us to God, being put to death in the flesh but made alive in the spirit, ¹⁹ in which he went and proclaimed to the spirits in prison,

Galatians 2:20 ²⁰ I have been crucified with Christ. It is no longer I who live, but Christ who lives in me. And the life I now live in the flesh I live by faith in the Son of God, who loved me and gave himself for me.

What to do next

I consider myself a student of life and a servant to all. I take on this roll so as to not let my ego grow. I need to remain humble and down to earth. I never want my ego to get out of control again. Be a good student and a servant too, thereby you too can remain humble. Be careful with what you say, and whose name you call for no reason. I use the example of crying wolf. I try to not say the expression of "Oh my God" or "Jesus Christ", as when I say it and I call on the lord, I want him to hear me and not treat my calling as a vain call. If all I did was call his name in vain what else might he expect? After all, it does say to not take the lords name in vain. Invest in yourself and continue to learn. Take the time to read more than just the passages I have copied into this book. When you read, do so with no preconceived notions so that the words can penetrate your heart. Know that by slowing down and observing your surroundings, you can gain wisdom and understanding simply by watching behaviors and studying patterns. When observing, be careful to see everything and all sides of any situation, not just what suits your perspective and do not judge. When you discover something new, carefully examine it by examining the feelings in your heart. Seek out truth and wisdom, there is an utter abundance available but know the right source to trust and where to find it. Pray and ask for more knowledge and wisdom, for the more you know and understand the easier it is to do what is right. The cleaner and purer your heart is, the more power you contain in your heart to receive what you ask for.

Mathew 7:8-11 *[8]* *For everyone who asks receives, and the one who seeks finds, and to the one who knocks it will be opened.* *[9]* *Or which one of you, if his son asks him for bread, will give him a stone?* *[10]* *Or if he asks for a fish, will give him a serpent?* *[11]* *If you then, who are evil, know how to give good gifts to your children, how much more will your Father who is in heaven give good things to those who ask him!*

Mathew 25:14-30 *[14]* *"For it will be like a man going on a journey, who called his servants and entrusted to them his property.* *[15]* *To one he gave five talents, to another two, to another one, to each according to his ability. Then he went away.* *[16]* *He who had received the five talents went at once and traded with them, and he made five talents more.* *[17]* *So also he who had the two talents made two talents more.* *[18]* *But he who had received the one talent went and dug in the ground and hid his master's money.* *[19]* *Now after a long time the master of those servants came and settled accounts with them.* *[20]* *And he who had received the five talents came forward, bringing five talents more, saying, 'Master, you delivered to me five talents; here I have made five talents more.'* *[21]* *His master said to him, 'Well done, good and faithful servant. You have been faithful over a little; I will set you over much. Enter into the joy of your master.'* *[22]* *And he also who had the two talents came forward, saying, 'Master, you delivered to me two talents; here I have made two talents more.'* *[23]* *His master said to him, 'Well done, good and faithful servant. You have been faithful over a little; I will set you over much. Enter into the joy of your master.'* *[24]* *He also who had received the one talent came forward, saying, 'Master, I knew you to be a hard man, reaping where you did not sow, and gathering where you scattered no seed,* *[25]* *so I was afraid, and I went and hid your talent in the ground. Here you have what is yours.'* *[26]* *But his master answered him, 'You wicked and slothful servant! You knew that I reap where I have not sown and gather where I scattered no seed?* *[27]* *Then you ought to have invested my money with the bankers, and at my coming I should have received what was my own with interest. ²⁸ So take the talent from him and give it to him who has the ten talents. ²⁹ For to everyone who has will more be given, and he will have an abundance. But from the one who has not, even what he has will be taken away. ³⁰ And cast the worthless servant into the outer darkness. In that place there will be weeping and gnashing of teeth.'*

Remember that in life sometimes in order to be fooled, someone may provide us with truth but sprinkle lies and deceitful teachings in with the truth. What I have found by looking into various alternate and new age spiritual programs is just that. To the newly lost trying to grow, it is quite tempting to follow. Without a good foundation in understanding the power and truth we have in Jesus Christ, many will be misled. Careful not to follow these teachings as they ultimately lead to death. If you understand that there is a force that is working against us trying to cause us to go off course in life by throwing road blocks and detours on the road, you can be smart and use the map provided in this book to avoid these traps. The enemy doesn't have to play fair, they only have one goal which is to destroy as many of us as possible. This is difficult for many to believe. It is difficult to accept that they have been deceived and are not following a path to light, the ego will do everything to blind them from understanding. The ego which grows in strength through identity and materialism will block the truth from penetrating their layers of dirt. Pray for them, that they will see the lies that they have put their faith in so they can alter their direction in life and find the right way. In the bible there are many passages predicting exactly this, take the time to read. Here is a couple to look at.

2 Corinthians 11:12-15 ¹² And what I am doing I will continue to do, in order to undermine the claim of those who would like to claim that in their boasted mission they work on the same terms as we do. ¹³ For such men are false apostles, deceitful workmen, disguising themselves as apostles of Christ. ¹⁴ *And no wonder, for even Satan disguises himself as an angel of light.* ¹⁵ *So it is no surprise if his servants, also, disguise themselves as servants of righteousness. Their end will correspond to their deeds.*

When you hear of people communicating with spirits in trances or using mediums to channel information, be vigilant and test the information and the source of the information. Does the knowledge seem to be mixed in with a lie? Does the knowledge go against the teachings in the bible? Draw on what you have learned so far, use your ability to pray and meditate on the subject before accepting the information as beneficial to staying on the right path. Weak minded people can be sold anything if they are told what they want to hear. People reaching out to loved ones that have passed on are extremely vulnerable as their emotions are broadcasting their thoughts loud and clear. They need to be extremely careful so as to not be fooled. Until you have built up such strength that you can no longer be fooled, it is best to stay away from these people. Do not let them infiltrate your thoughts. Protect your thoughts and beliefs with the words of wisdom found in the bible. Be strong and use the word of God as a shield by relying on the knowledge and wisdom provided in the bible. It is too easy to follow someone when they are buying you through lies. When they are offering you the very thing your flesh or ego desires which is normally identity and materialism, look for truth and guidance. We are given tools to know a good spirit from a bad spirit, bad spirits cannot confess that Jesus Christ is lord for in so doing, they humbly submit to his authority. Know this to be true, for many spirits will try to be clever when channeling. They try to trick everyone and will construct the reference to Jesus Christ in a way that they do not actually confess that Jesus Christ is lord. For example, I watched a program documentary where the medium kept saying, "The man you call Jesus Christ".

In other words, the spirit that was channeled would not submit to stating Jesus Christ is lord. References to this can be found all over the bible, here is a few passages.

1 Corinthians 12:1-11 Now concerning spiritual gifts, brethren, I do not want you to be ignorant: [2] You know that you were Gentiles, carried away to these dumb idols, however you were led. [3] Therefore I make known to you that no one speaking by the Spirit of God calls Jesus accursed, and no one can say that Jesus is Lord except by the Holy Spirit.

1 John 4:1-6 [1]Beloved, do not believe every spirit, but test the spirits to see whether they are from God, for many false prophets have gone out into the world. [2] By this you know the Spirit of God: every spirit that confesses that Jesus Christ has come in the flesh is from God, [3] and every spirit that does not confess Jesus is not from God. This is the spirit of the antichrist, which you heard was coming and now is in the world already. [4] Little children, you are from God and have overcome them, for he who is in you is greater than he who is in the world. [5] They are from the world; therefore they speak from the world, and the world listens to them. [6] We are from God. Whoever knows God listens to us; whoever is not from God does not listen to us. By this we know the Spirit of truth and the spirit of error.

Something we all want to have a better understanding is to define what God is, I tell you that it is something we each can feel if we search within ourselves. This requires us to slow down and look within to find God, through prayer and meditation you will come to know the truth. In order to meditate, we need to learn how to tell that voice in our head to be quiet so that we can listen. I tell you that the greatest tool the devil has is its ability to keep many people on the hamster wheel, running and running to nowhere. These negative energies cause stress in life and make us feel that we need to hurry and get somewhere all the time. It fools us into keeping us busy so we naturally will make excuses why we can't take the time to slow down. It is easier to make the excuse that we cannot pray or meditate, but know that is not our true self. That is the ego controlling your actions. These negative energies tug at our ego knowing that our ego is willing to do anything to avoid you seeing the truth. Don't allow yourself to be tricked, be smart and take control of the ego. In summary, by providing for layers of identification through the ego and a desire to obtain as much materialistic things as possible we end up living in a stress latent lifestyle that tricks us into believing we have no time for slowing down in order to reflect, meditate and pray. The trick many fall for is in the attachment to the desires of the flesh. The ego and materialistic things we have gained or want to gain keep us in constant check through fear of losing them if we were to slow down. Amazing how we can fall into such a trap as to not know God and live for the materialistic world. Here are a couple passages on who is God and dangers of living for the flesh, ego or materialism. Please, there is many more and I ask that you take it upon yourself to read on.

1 John 4:7-11 7 Beloved, let us love one another, for love is from God, and whoever loves has been born of God and knows God. 8 Anyone who does not love does not know God, because God is love. 9 In this the love of God was made manifest among us, that God sent his only Son into the world, so that we might live through him. 10 In this is love, not that we have loved God but that he loved us and sent his Son to be the propitiation for our sins. 11 Beloved, if God so loved us, we also ought to love one another. 12 No one has ever seen God; if we love one another, God abides in us and his love is perfected in us.

Romans 8:12-14 12 So then, brothers, we are debtors, not to the flesh, to live according to the flesh. 13 For if you live according to the flesh you will die, but if by the Spirit you put to death the deeds of the body, you will live. 14 For all who are led by the Spirit of God are sons of God.

I want you to understand why it is important to surround yourself with people, places and things that emanate good energy. As your eyes open and you wake up, you will see all around us the materialism that is robbing people of their very souls. Even when they are presented with the factual evidence, their own ego for fear of losing stuff they cannot keep and take with them when they leave the physical world, will block them from accepting the truth. I want to make sure you know that the ego will do everything it can to distort the truth and prevent anyone from hearing and listening if they lose control of the ego. It will do everything it can to keep anyone from accumulating real wealth in the form of spiritual gifts. The ego grows with identification and materialism. We have all grown up to misunderstand its influence over us and therefore it is causing us to have a distorted view of the truth. In my quests, I worked with many good people who seem to be stuck in their spiritual growth as they are trying to heal. Evidence of this can be found in the infusion of reward or recognition programs that allow for one to boast and grow their ego within programs designed to remove the self centeredness that nurtures the ego. Rather than looking at their own spiritual growth, they weigh heavily on the illusion of time as a measure of spiritual growth. Some wear this badge of honor and value it too much. In so doing, they unknowingly allow themselves to be lied to while the ego and materialism grows in the background ready to pounce when the time is right. Some build such a superiority complex that they actually hurt people by holding them down and by belittling someone new. Not all fall into this trap, but many do. I have even been witness to those that build up new jealous resentments about people they are supposed to be friends with or helping. They then hold this as a secret within the program. Secrets, resentments and hate are dangerous as they erode the container they are held in, the heart. Many also are stuck in the inability to open their eyes to more truths, truths that come from the best source of all wisdom, the bible. They limit what they will allow themselves to absorb out of fear.

It is difficult at first glance to see what is happening, but again if you look carefully you will see the truth. If they opened their eyes by observing the structure as a whole and see the hypocrisy in the philosophies, what a difference it would make in the time it takes to heal. In understanding the importance to deflate or eliminate the ego, then it is not possible to believe that by offering ways that allows for individuals to have separate levels of identities or to accumulate rewards and recognition in a way that designates a methodology that incorporates measuring, it is dangerous. Anything that could be used by an individual to gauge an attitude of superiority over another person will lead to individualism, the need for identity and re-growth of the ego. In other words, by encouraging this reward type of behavior, it is fostering a way for the ego to grow within and directly underneath the programs very nose. I do not want to belittle the numerous program benefits at work. The significant benefits these programs offer as a way to introduce many into what spirituality is and to get a chance to understand and begin a relationship with God is remarkable. Within these programs, there are many that do understand the dilemma of rewards and the need for the elimination of the ego. Those are the sources of wisdom in those groups that can help guide others just beginning their journey. They have a much wider grasp of wisdom, the key here is to know how to take from it the good components and leave the rest as the rest falls under the 80/20 rule I have already discussed. I only mention this to you, so that if you do see or get involved with other facets or ways of trying to improve your understanding you will know to steer clear of these stumbling blocks. It seems that indeed, some force is always trying to infiltrate and confuse the thinking in a manner that can breed its limiting restrictions even within programs designed to help. The idea of receiving too many rewards and praise for doing something right is what you must always look out for, as that again is a subtle way the ego finds its way back in to fester and grow. What a difference it would make if they understood how the lure of praise when doing something right is a desire of the ego. This is why I strive to be a student always willing to learn and a humble servant always willing to serve. I pray that I remain strong in this regard.

I do not want to go back to discussing too much about the ego, but some things I should include as it relates to what I want you to understand. Realize that a fallacy is that the ego has to do with only reward and identification with positive things. That is not true, for if someone has identified themselves with negative things it can be just as bad and dangerous. The ego can feed off and grow through identification with either good or bad identification or labels of self. For example, the person who always states they are fat, or ugly, or the person who is trapped into certain patterns of behavior. All these things can let the ego grow and form protective layers of identification that can make it difficult for even sound truth to penetrate and enter the heart.

Until the realization to who you really are has been set in your heart, stay away from the people with strong egos. Know that in extreme cases those with very strong egos reach levels of what psychiatrist themselves attribute and label to as narcissistic and sociopathic behaviors. When they reach these levels, they are so disconnected with reality that they believe they are being controlled by others, so much so that they act out so defiantly against everyone and anyone who does not agree with them. The very thing they seek, which is to not be controlled is the very thing they lost. They have no self control anymore over anything. They are at the mercy of emotions. They react to everything in life and consequently they cannot see that they lost control of their behavior by satisfying certain emotional and physical needs, they are indeed being controlled by everyone and everything around them. The emotions generated through their feeling and how they interpret the reality around them, cause them to act out in ways that defy common logic and sound reasoning. I use the term interpret, as it is truly the perspective they feel and once they are in this sick and twisted state, it is difficult to admit they are wrong. They believe their perception of the situation is true and so their feelings are accurate and therefore the reaction to the situation is justified. It is a vicious cycle that one can lead themselves into and feel trapped if they do not know what tools are available that can be used to escape the grip of insanity. I see this happening more and more often, for I too was falling into this trap at one point in my life, so be on guard and aware of them. Here is a great passage that talks about what we can expect as we approach the end of the age.

2 Timothy 3:1-9 ¹ But understand this, that in the last days there will come times of difficulty. ² For people will be lovers of self, lovers of money, proud, arrogant, abusive, disobedient to their parents, ungrateful, unholy, ³ heartless, unappeasable, slanderous, without self-control, brutal, not loving good, ⁴ treacherous, reckless, swollen with conceit, lovers of pleasure rather than lovers of God, ⁵ having the appearance of godliness, but denying its power. Avoid such people. ⁶ For among them are those who creep into households and capture weak women, burdened with sins and led astray by various passions, ⁷ always learning and never able to arrive at a knowledge of the truth. ⁸ Just as Jannes and Jambres opposed Moses, so these men also oppose the truth, men corrupted in mind and disqualified regarding the faith. ⁹ But they will not get very far, for their folly will be plain to all, as was that of those two men.

I want to share with you some other insights with you that if taken for face value, with show the truth behind the statement on its own merit. For instance, if you want to know the condition of the society in which a person lives, simply look at the number of laws they have on the books. You see laws are for the unjust, the disobedient, the liars and thieves. A righteous person does not need law to know what is right and wrong, they just know and always choose to do what is right. Laws are for controlling those individuals or groups that are morally bankrupt. The laws are to protect those people or groups that are good in nature and have strong morals from those that are morally bankrupt. If a truly righteous person ever wonders about a choice or decision, they can rely on the "What would Jesus do" or the Golden rule from principle three. If you look at the amount of laws we have on the books just to keep society in order, you can guess the condition of our state of being. Here is an excerpt that clearly demonstrates what I am trying to explain.

1 Timothy 1:8-10 [8] *Now we know that the law is good, if one uses it lawfully,* [9] *understanding this, that the law is not laid down for the just but for the lawless and disobedient, for the ungodly and sinners, for the unholy and profane, for those who strike their fathers and mothers, for murderers,* [10] *the sexually immoral, men who practice homosexuality, enslavers, liars, perjurers, and whatever else is contrary to sound doctrine,* [11] *in accordance with the gospel of the glory of the blessed God with which I have been entrusted.*

I want to touch on some other less popular topics that you may not be ready to understand just yet but is important. The importance of morality in relationship to sexual behavior is extremely important. Remaining pure is best and abstinence and there are reasons for it. I will not get into all of them. I will touch on just a few. Those that retain virginity have retained all their purity and spirit, they have not released their energy and become unclean. By unleashing this desire, you continually pour out your energy.

This energy has the power to create and destroy. If the energy is contained and used to connect spiritually to God and each other the right way, it can create. When the energy is unleashed through sexual activity, it will strip you completely of your energy eventually and you lose your spiritual connection to God and each other. You inevitably grow desires of the flesh that can never be truly satisfied when it grows out of immortality. Those that partake in this activity immorally and often, completely lose their connection to God. They lose their ability to sense the presence of God spiritually. These people always question the existence as they can longer perceive God directly. They fell into a trap, where they chase the physical sensation seeking immediate satisfaction and in so doing they give up their energy and quickly, especially when done often and outside of marriage. There are documents on the correct methods of practicing sexual behavior and you can find them if you search. I have heard of practicing white tantric as a method as it is considered pure as no energy wasted and released. Black and grey tantric practices can lead to spiritual disconnection, but I will leave these various methods for you to research. What is important here is to remain sexually moral.

For your reference, I have copied in a couple passages on the importance of sexual morality. By far, these are not the only references to these topics in the bible, so please do you own research as they are very important when you are navigating your way through life. Again, do not judge others for we each have our own demons to overcome. Be aware of these stumbling blocks, steer clear of those participating in these actions and be thankful that we are given an opportunity to be freed of sin.

1 Corinthians 6:9-10 ⁹ Or do you not know that the unrighteous will not inherit the kingdom of God? Do not be deceived: neither the sexually immoral, nor idolaters, nor adulterers, nor men who practice homosexuality,

¹⁰ nor thieves, nor the greedy, nor drunkards, nor revilers, nor swindlers will inherit the kingdom of God.

1 Corinthians 6:18-20 ¹⁸ Flee from sexual immorality. Every other sin a person commits is outside the body, but the sexually immoral person sins against his own body. ¹⁹ Or do you not know that your body is a temple of the Holy Spirit within you, whom you have from God? You are not your own, ²⁰ for you were bought with a price. So glorify God in your body.

How we, the rest of us received salvation was due to the Jews steadfast hardheadedness in past times. I want to point out this unique passage that explains this clearly and it is long, but it required most of this section to be copied from the bible to explain it clearly. Please take the time to read more about this.

Romans 11:1-24 ¹ I ask, then, has God rejected his people? By no means! For I myself am an Israelite, a descendant of Abraham, a member of the tribe of Benjamin. ² God has not rejected his people whom he foreknew. Do you not know what the Scripture says of Elijah, how he appeals to God against Israel? ³ "Lord, they have killed your prophets, they have demolished your altars, and I alone am left, and they seek my life." ⁴ But what is God's reply to him? "I have kept for myself seven thousand men who have not bowed the knee to Baal." ⁵ So too at the present time there is a remnant, chosen by grace. ⁶ But if it is by grace, it is no longer on the basis of works; otherwise grace would no longer be grace.

⁷ What then? Israel failed to obtain what it was seeking. The elect obtained it, but the rest were hardened, ⁸ as it is written,

"God gave them a spirit of stupor,
  eyes that would not see
  and ears that would not hear,
  down to this very day."

⁹ And David says,

"Let their table become a snare and a trap,
  a stumbling block and a retribution for them;
¹⁰ let their eyes be darkened so that they cannot see,
  and bend their backs forever."

¹¹ So I ask, did they stumble in order that they might fall? By no means! Rather through their trespass salvation has come to the Gentiles, so as to make Israel jealous. ¹² Now if their trespass means riches for the world, and if their failure means riches for the Gentiles, how much more will their full inclusion mean!

¹³ Now I am speaking to you Gentiles. Inasmuch then as I am an apostle to the Gentiles, I magnify my ministry ¹⁴ in order somehow to make my fellow Jews jealous, and thus save some of them. ¹⁵ For if their rejection means the reconciliation of the world, what will their acceptance mean but life from the dead? ¹⁶ If the dough offered as firstfruits is holy, so is the whole lump, and if the root is holy, so are the branches.

¹⁷ But if some of the branches were broken off, and you, although a wild olive shoot, were grafted in among the others and now share in the nourishing root of the olive tree, ¹⁸ do not be arrogant toward the branches. If you are, remember it is not you who support the root, but the root that supports you. ¹⁹ Then you will say, "Branches were broken off so that I might be grafted in." ²⁰ That is true. They were broken off because of their unbelief, but you stand fast through faith. So do not become proud, but fear. ²¹ For if God did not spare the natural branches, neither will he spare you. ²² Note then the kindness and the severity of God: severity toward those who have fallen, but God's kindness to you, provided you continue in his kindness. Otherwise you too will be cut off. ²³ And even they, if they do not continue in their unbelief, will be grafted in, for God has the power to graft them in again. ²⁴ For if you were cut from what is by nature

a wild olive tree, and grafted, contrary to nature, into a cultivated olive tree, how much more will these, the natural branches, be grafted back into their own olive tree.

I want to add to this, that we must pray for Israel as they are not cut-off from God by any stretch of the imagination. They will survive and we must support them. In many places in the bible this is made evidently clear, but none so much as the continuation of this passage below. We therefore need to remember always how important it is to support them.

Romans 11:25-26 [25] Lest you be wise in your own sight, I do not want you to be unaware of this mystery, brothers: a partial hardening has come upon Israel, until the fullness of the Gentiles has come in. [26] And in this way all Israel will be saved, as it is written,

"The Deliverer will come from Zion,
  he will banish ungodliness from Jacob";

We have to remember that everything is connected so everything that happens in the physical word affects the spiritual word and everything that happens in the spiritual words affect the physical world. We see rituals designed to bring together changes in consciousness both good and bad. There is no such thing as coincidence and everything happens for a reason. We are all interconnected in some way. We try to achieve the spiritual reconnection in many ways. One way we practice this in the physical is through the practice of Holy Matrimony where a male and a female are united as one and they create a child. The goal is to spiritually unite ourselves into one again. The secret is talked about in metaphors, where the bride and the bridegroom are united in the bridal chamber. The reconnection of the feminine and masculine into one is the goal. In the reconnection, a child is created. The practice is done mentally in a way. Some would best describe it occurring at a different frequency through deep meditation where you achieve a trance like state. We need to reunite our male and female aspects in our mind. A mind without a heart is heartless and lacking warmth and affection. A heart without a mind is lacking reason and meaning. The left side of the brain is considered masculine and logical thinking and the right side of the brain is feminine and is connected to the heart and is composed of love and feelings. The goal is to unite them. There is plenty of information to help you achieve this feat and that is best discovered on your own when you are ready.

I want to bring up another unpopular topic. If we look around us, there are signs that we as a society are progressing down a road that is not in our best interest. We are being provided ample warning time so that we can all wake up and make a course correction as a society. We cannot know for certainty when the end of time is at hand, for only God knows that. What we can do is look at the clues left behind and compare it to our current surroundings and see if anything fits. Unless God wants us to know, we will not know for certainty as is it stated many times in the bible that the end will come like a thief in the night and to be on guard.

We can see that God has slowly been removed from our culture under the pretense of separation for the purpose of guaranteeing religious freedom. We are told that removing references to God anywhere the government is involved is the best way to promote religious freedom. The judges that made these ruling were asleep. Any philosophy that follows the suppression of God, whether it be under the umbrella of an agnostic or atheist belief is in fact a religious belief. In other words, by the very act that a belief is declared in relation to the existence of God even if that belief is the denial of God, the core structure of the belief has been stated which is to not believe in a single or any God. The government made a ruling to remove God from Schools or and any government sponsored activity, therefore they have indeed supported a religion where God does not exist. This is hypocrisy. The only way to stay neutral and not be involved would be to have done nothing and let each group, organization, school or whatever decide for themselves whether they would offer prayer as an option for those that wanted to join in. By making a ruling to prevent and not permit prayer publicly in school or anywhere they are suppressing it, they have indeed adhered to a religion whereby the philosophy and the belief of the religion is based upon living without God.

Another more obvious action is the involvement of the governments in religious affairs terminology and meaning. Their action in supporting the re-definition of marriage by giving into pressure to allow for two people of the same sex to be accepted as being married is dangerous. They call this politics, where you give a little to get a little. Acting morally wrong to gain identity and power does not serve anything but oneself. I use this one simple action as an example, but there are many. Overstepping their authority to try and alter certain universally accepted laws whereby marriage of two into one has always been defined as a balance of the female and male energies in a sacred union is not a good thing at all. That sacred union requires a male and a female. Therefore in their actions, by accepting the request to change the definition of marriage it is as though they have entered into an agreement that may lead to the opening of Pandora's box. They actually have not changed anything, as man does not dictate the universal laws anyway and a true marriage is between a male and a female. It does not work any other way. You cannot hold anything together with two bolts or two nuts. You need a nut and a bolt to unite something. It is simple to understand, as above so below. Don't over complicate things, keep it simple. The issue is that by the governments taking this action to allow for gay marriage, they have provided for acceptance of sexual immorality at a large scale, therefore propagating lies that it is ok to act in this way. This is not my opinion as it comes from a higher authority. Stay away from these situations as best as you can and at the same time, do not judge their behaviors, as that is for God to do. Treat all your interaction with other people with respect, regardless of whether you think they are doing good or not. Remember you have the choice to determine who or what you will surround yourself with. Make wise choices. Take the time to just read how often the union of the male and female into one is described in the bible, here is just a couple passages.

1 Corinthians 7:2 ² *But because of the temptation to sexual immorality, each man should have his own wife and each woman her own husband.*

Hebrews 13:4 ⁴ *Let marriage be held in honor among all, and let the marriage bed be undefiled, for God will judge the sexually immoral and adulterous.*

Remember the bible as the true source that contains deep wisdom and knowledge on all these things I want you to be aware of. Read and study the bible, for there is much to be deciphered and perhaps you may realize something I did not. Don't be pulled away by the distractions of daily life, as that is a subtle approach used to put you on the wrong path or delay you from continuing down the right way. Take the time to slow down and let this information seep deep within you, that it may grow and receive the proper nurturing for it will keep you safe. Think about the next passage from the bible and read further into them for if you truly seek out the wisdom, it will be given to you.

Luke 17:24-32 [24] *For as the lightning flashes and lights up the sky from one side to the other, so will the Son of Man be in his day.* [25] *But first he must suffer many things and be rejected by this generation.* [26] *Just as it was in the days of Noah, so will it be in the days of the Son of Man.* [27] *They were eating and drinking and marrying and being given in marriage, until the day when Noah entered the ark, and the flood came and destroyed them all.* [28] *Likewise, just as it was in the days of Lot—they were eating and drinking, buying and selling, planting and building,* [29] *but on the day when Lot went out from Sodom, fire and sulfur rained from heaven and destroyed them all—* [30] *so will it be on the day when the Son of Man is revealed.* [31] *On that day, let the one who is on the housetop, with his goods in the house, not come down to take them away, and likewise let the one who is in the field not turn back.* [32] *Remember Lot's wife.*

The most important thing now is whether this was enough to change your mind and if so did it get past all the layers of the ego and past all the materialism so that it settles deep within your heart where it will grow. Realizing that growth can be exponentially faster when properly nurtured, you would want to continue feeding it in different ways. What I mean by that is surrounding yourself in the right environment where it can be fertilized. Stay away from circumstances that can poison what you have planted so far. Steer clear of situations that you know are questionable or may have an adverse effect on the direction you are heading in life. Below is parable from the bible that I have copied in for you to read that does a far better job explaining what to look out for and how to insure you will stay on the course.

Luke 8:4-15 [4] *And when a great crowd was gathering and people from town after town came to him, he said in a parable,* [5] *"A sower went out to sow his seed. And as he sowed, some fell along the path and was trampled underfoot, and the birds of the air devoured it.* *⁶And some fell on the rock, and as it grew up, it withered away, because it had no moisture.* *⁷And some fell among thorns, and the thorns grew up with it and choked it.* *⁸And some fell into good soil and grew and yielded a hundredfold." As he said these things, he called out, "He who has ears to hear, let him hear."* *⁹And when his disciples asked him what this parable meant,* *¹⁰he said, "To you it has been given to know the secrets of the kingdom of God, but for others they are in parables, so that 'seeing they may not see, and hearing they may not understand.'* *¹¹Now the parable is this: The seed is the word of God.* *¹²The ones along the path are those who have heard; then the devil comes and takes away the word from their hearts, so that they may not believe and be saved.* *¹³And the ones on the rock are those who, when they hear the word, receive it with joy. But these have no root; they believe for a while, and in time of testing fall away.* *¹⁴And as for what fell among the thorns, they are those who hear, but as they go on their way they are choked by the cares and riches and pleasures of life, and their fruit does not mature.* *¹⁵As for that in the good soil, they are those who, hearing the word, hold it fast in an honest and good heart, and bear fruit with patience.*

I sincerely hope that by gathering and organizing the major philosophies into these three core principles, you will gain a strong foundation on how to live life the right way. I hope and pray that I have found a way to pierce through the multiple layers of your ego so that the truth that can set you free enters your heart, where it belongs. That you will be able to minimize the layers of ego so that you will experience minimal or no suffering if God so blesses you that way. That the truth continues to grow inside you so that by growing, it drives out any evil or negative energies that try to enter. There has always been an interesting question I have seen everywhere and never really understood its significance but now I do. I copied it from the bible so as not to mistranslate it in any way.

Mathew 16:24-26 [24] *Then Jesus told his disciples, "If anyone would come after me, let him deny himself and take up his cross and follow me.* [25] *For whoever would save his life will lose it, but whoever loses his life for my sake will find it.* [26] *For what will it profit a man if he gains the whole world and forfeits his soul? Or what shall a man give in return for his soul?*

In the end, what is important to know is that there are forces that try to pull you away. Realizing the different ways that these forces materialize and can influence you can help you to gain a better understanding on ways to protect yourself. Not knowing these forces even exist, is like constantly being robbed and never knowing it until you are bankrupt. By being aware that these forces do not play fair, that they usually hide and do not make themselves consciously known, you will be better able to recognize what is going on in your life to better safeguard yourself from future attacks. Sometimes these forces can overpower the people around you. If those people are ill prepared, the forces may try to use them to get to you as they are trying to pull you away from the truth. Do not be discouraged, pray for them that they can see and understand through their own experiences the truth as to what is going on. Have a clear intention to be good and strive to always do what is right, no matter what feeling or emotion is welling up in your body. It is best to not make decisions based upon irrational emotional states of mind.

Many of the spiritual programs offered similar advice in regards to the ego and materialism. They talked about things like energy centers that work in conjunction with the body, called chakras. I can sum it all up that there are energies all around us and we need to stay clear of certain traps. You want to stay clear of anything that traps you into the desires of material word. There are three basic forms of attachment to the physical world that keep us from ascending to a higher spiritual existence that we all must overcome.

1) Attached to materialistic world through desires of the flesh. This could be physical feelings, like food, drugs, gambling or sex or feelings that emanate from owning materialistic things and a strong desire for money.

2) Attached to identify through a strong EGO. This is when you are afraid to show who you really are to the people around you for fear of what they may think. You may hide true beliefs and act differently around different people rather than being who you really are.

3) Attached due to be owed a debt of some sort. This is when you do wrong to others or have been wronged and you hold resentment(s). By not forgiving someone of their debt or not being forgiven for your debt to someone else will keep you attached as everyone has to make good on their obligations. It must balance and no debt obligation can be unsatisfied, but they can be forgiven.

I came up with some little basic prayers I sometimes say to help keep me on the right path once I discovered that I had been unknowingly led the wrong way and was lost. I was concerned as to why I wanted to change and I wanted my motives to be pure, so I added them into my prayers that if any part of my reasoning was not right and just, to change it for me. You can create your own, these are just examples of what I will pray for sometimes.

Lord, I ask that you help me to be true to your word. That I seek honestly and righteousness for the right reasons and if there is any desire in me that is seeking to achieve cleanliness and forgiveness for the wrong reason, that you change it for me so that my thoughts and my heart are in harmony with what you want for me. I ask that no matter what challenges in life I face, that you keep me from going astray. I ask that you give me patience and compassion, so that even though I may not understand why I have to face specific challenges in my life, I do it knowing that you always have my best interest in mind. I ask that you help me remain a humble servant, open to recognizing my faults so that I can be a good student always willing to learn more and better myself. Amen

Lord, I ask that I forgive everyone for everything and that I be forgiven for my own faults. That I no longer sin, that I become free and continue to be free and willingly turn my will over to you. And if there is someone or some circumstance that I am holding onto resentment(s) in any shape or form or not forgiving some trespass against me, that you please show it to me and help me forgive unconditionally so that I can be free to serve you. I ask that regardless the circumstance you allow to enter into my life, that I remain faithful to your word. I ask that you help me remain a humble servant, open to recognizing my faults so that I can be a good student always willing to learn more and better myself. Amen

St. Francis was my confirmation Saint, here is
his Prayer. His prayer has so much wisdom and
truth contained within a few simple words.

St. Francis Prayer

Lord, make me a channel of thy peace,
that where there is hatred, I may bring love;
that where there is wrong, I may bring the spirit of forgiveness;
that where there is discord, I may bring harmony;
that where there is error, I may bring truth;
that where there is doubt, I may bring faith;
that where there is despair, I may bring hope;
that where there are shadows, I may bring light;
that where there is sadness, I may bring joy.
Lord, grant that I may seek rather to
comfort than to be comforted;
to understand, than to be understood;
to love, than to be loved.
For it is by self-forgetting that one finds.
It is by forgiving that one is forgiven.
It is by dying that one awakens to Eternal Life.